UNDAUNTED

OTHER BOOKS
BY ALAN TWIGG

The Essentials: 150 Great BC Books & Authors (Ronsdale, 2010)

Tibetans in Exile: The Dalai Lama & The Woodcocks
(Ronsdale, 2009)

Full-Time: A Soccer Story
(Douglas Gibson Books, McClelland & Stewart, 2008)

Thompson's Highway: British Columbia's Fur Trade,
1800–1850 (Ronsdale, 2006)

Understanding Belize: A Historical Guide (Harbour, 2006)

Aboriginality: The Literary Origins of British Columbia
(Ronsdale, 2005)

First Invaders: The Literary Origins of British Columbia
(Ronsdale, 2004)

101 Top Historical Sites of Cuba (Beach Holme, 2004)

Intensive Care: A Memoir (Anvil Press, 2002)

Cuba: A Concise History for Travellers (Harbour, 2004; Penguin
Books, 2002; Bluefield Books 2000)

Twigg's Directory of 1001 BC Writers (Crown Publications, 1992)

Strong Voices: Conversations with 50 Canadian Writers
(Harbour, 1988)

Vander Zalm, From Immigrant to Premier: A Political Biography
(Harbour, 1986)

Vancouver and Its Writers (Harbour, 1986)

Hubert Evans: The First Ninety-Three Years (Harbour, 1985)

For Openers: Conversations with 24 Canadian Writers
(Harbour, 1981)

UNDAUNTED
THE BEST OF BC BOOKWORLD

Edited by
Alan Twigg

Illustrations by
David Lester

RONSDALE PRESS

RONSDALE PRESS
3350 West 21st Avenue
Vancouver, B.C. Canada V6S 1G7
www.ronsdalepress.com

Typesetting: Julie Cochrane, in Granjon 11.5 pt on 15
Cover Design: David Lester
Copy Editors: Deirdre Salisbury & Meagan Dyer
Paper: Ancient Forest Friendly 55lb "Silva" (FSC) — 100% post-consumer waste, totally chlorine-free and acid-free.

Ronsdale Press wishes to thank the following for their support of its publishing program: the Canada Council for the Arts, the Government of Canada through the Canada Book Fund, the British Columbia Arts Council, and the Province of British Columbia through the British Columbia Book Publishing Tax Credit program.

Library and Archives Canada Cataloguing in Publication

Undaunted: the best of BC bookworld / edited by Alan Twigg.

Includes index.
A compilation of articles and essays from the quarterly newspaper, BC bookworld.
Includes 25 cartoons by David Lester.
Preface by Howard White.
Issued in print and electronic formats.
ISBN 978-1-55380-253-2 (print)
ISBN 978-1-55380-254-9 (ebook) / ISBN 978-1-55380-255-6 (pdf)

1. Canadian essays (English) — 21st century. I. Twigg, Alan, 1952–, editor of compilation II. White, Howard, 1945–, writer of added commentary III. Title: Best of BC bookworld.

PS8373.1.B33 2013   C808.84'9971   C2013-903233-9
                                              C2013-903234-7

Printed in Canada by Marquis Book Printing, Quebec

In memory of

Jane Rule

and

George Woodcock

ACKNOWLEDGEMENTS

Thanks to Ebony Magnus for collating this manuscript and her editorial input. Thanks to David Lester for his unfailing partnership and friendship. Thanks to all the writers who have contributed during our first twenty-five years. Thanks to you, the reader — the most important person in the mix.

Contents

SECTION 4: Writing in BC

SECTION 5: Potpourri

Preface

~ HOWARD WHITE

IT IS WELL KNOWN THAT *BC BookWorld* is an indispensable reference for readers of books by BC authors and a certified West Coast institution, but something that may not be as well known and which this book proves, is that this self-described "populist newspaper" has published much original writing that is engaging and memorable.

BookWorld's promethean editor, Alan Twigg, is himself a writer of numerous BC books, and as BC Lit's chief cheerleader he has made it his business to sneak in well-authored essays on a mind-boggling array of subjects whenever he's had the chance. And he has had many chances over the 25 years that *BC BookWorld* has been serving as the publication of record for everything that appears under the rubric of BC literature.

The list of contributors to this book includes many of BC's most distinguished writers, including the venerable poet Lionel Kearns; the groundbreaking lesbian novelist Jane Rule; the literary boulevardier Stephen

Vizinczey; the Leakey's Angel Biruté Galdikas; the "Chomsky of Kitsilano," Joel Bakan; the Coast Lit maven Charles Lillard; the Field of Dreams originator W.P. Kinsella; the First Nations statesman Chief Joe Gosnell; the immaculate punster Eric Nicol; the twin towers of Canadian bestsellerdom Pierre Berton and Peter Newman; the gentleman of letters Robin Skelton paying tribute to the colossus of letters George Woodcock, as well as the colossus himself in his own write.

The range of topics essayed by these worthies is charmingly random. Kearns relates a remarkable anecdote in which he, as an unassuming student on a work visit to Cuba in the 1960s, ended up as catcher in a game of pick-up baseball in which the pitcher was none other than Fidel Castro himself. Castro, he reports, had good stuff but refused to obey signals. Jane Rule talks about her lifelong struggle to establish herself as a writer free of the labels "American," "Canadian," "feminist," "lesbian," and indeed, even "writer" in a funny and brilliant piece that is worth the price of admission by itself. Fearless Stephen Vizinczey uses a volume of Vladimir Nabokov's letters as a springboard to ambush the great man himself, pronouncing Nabokov petty, artificial and narrow. Biruté Galdikas, who has spent much of her life in the jungles of Borneo enlarging our knowledge of orangutans, decries the global economy's reckless plunge into the future "like a high-speed locomotive with no one at the controls," and explains why humans should care about saving their great ape siblings. Joel Bakan, the sober and civilized UBC professor who wrote the bestselling polemic *The Corporation*, contributes a hair-raising tale of venturing into the tinsel jungles of the film industry.

Twigg's approach to criticism is apparent in the rich texture of this collection. He sees books as so many windows on the world, and he reviews them by evoking the worlds they contain, sometimes more vividly than the original authors. This saves his own numerous contributions to *Undaunted* from any hint of repetitiveness. Their one thread is that they are all inspired by books written by someone who lives or once lived in BC, but beyond that they tackle every topic under the sun. He shifts from a reconsideration of Malinche, the Indian woman behind Cortés' conquest of Mexico, to a little-known Tsawwassen woman named Louise Jilek-Aal whose books are about working as a bush doctor in Tanzania and serving as an assistant to Albert Schweitzer. His review of a book by historian Barry Gough gives new life to the legend of Juan de Fuca, the 16th-century Greek pilot who may have discovered BC; his reading of Jim McDowell's *Hamatsa* provides a fascinating summary of the argument about whether or not aboriginal groups along the BC coast practised cannibalism before the coming of Europeans, and his examination of Becki L. Ross' *Burlesque West: Showgirls, Sex and Sin in Postwar Vancouver* provides an eye-opening expose of No-fun City's hidden history as a mecca of erotic dancing.

In all of these articles, the editor and his contributors open the covers of significant BC books and let them speak for themselves. In that way *Undaunted: The Best of BC BookWorld* is a rich tasting menu of some of the most compelling books written by British Columbians over the last 25 years.

This is a very robust mixture that makes clear, whatever real and imagined challenges the book business may face worldwide, here on the West Coast writers forge ahead undaunted.

— HOWARD WHITE, president,
Pacific BookWorld News Society

SECTION 1

International

The Day I Caught Fidel

⟿ LIONEL KEARNS

■ Teacher and poet Lionel Kearns is, among other things, also the only British Columbian to have played a full game of baseball with Fidel Castro in Cuba during the 1960s. Here, Kearns describes how, on a student work trip to Cuba only three years after the Cuban Missile Crisis, he found himself playing ball with Castro, a skilled pitcher who cared little for taking direction from others, including his catcher.

"YOU CAN'T PLAY BALL with the Commies" — that's what they used to say when I was a kid growing up in a little town in the interior of British Columbia. They weren't really talking about baseball. It had more to do with Igor Gouzenko's defection in Canada, Joe McCarthy's witch hunts in the US and that big shift in attitude that went with the Cold War.

But there I was, a few years later, squatting behind the plate, squinting through the bars of a catcher's mask, the sweat running down into my eyes, as Fidel Castro fired the old *pelota* down on me from the pitcher's mound in the sports stadium of Santiago de Cuba.

It was the summer of 1964. I was en route to London on a Common-wealth Scholarship, with a few stopovers along the way. Some weeks earlier I had been staying with my old poetry buddy, George Bowering, in Mexico City. He and his wife Angela had rented a little apartment on *Avenida Béisbol*. Baseball Street! How was I going to top that one?

I had come to Mexico to join a group of other students from various parts of Canada. We had all signed up to participate in a work project in Cuba, but there were no direct flights from Canada at that time. Three years after the Missile Crisis and two years after the abortive US-sponsored Bay of Pigs invasion, Cuba was not a popular tourist destination. However, we found the island full of students from all over the world. Some of them were studying at Cuban schools and universities, and some, like us, had come for shorter visits, invited by the government to witness the Revolution first hand, in order to counter the bad image it was getting in the Western press.

The American blockade of the island was still in effect. We could see the US warships on the horizon when we walked down the Malecón on the Havana sea front. US fighter jets buzzed the city every day or two just to shake things up, and U-2 spy planes flew high overhead. On the ground there wasn't much food or luxury, but there was great enthusiasm.

Our group spent a week in Havana and then began moving east through the island, sometimes in a green Czech bus, sometimes in the rusty bucket of a big Russian dump truck. Other international student *invitados*, including a group of Americans, were doing the same kind of thing. We would meet them here and there along the way. Everywhere the Cubans welcomed us, and told us about what was happening and what they were experiencing and expecting. I was glad that I could speak Spanish.

As it turned out, we did not make it to the cane fields. Instead, we spent a week doing manual labour on a school construction site in the Sierra Maestra Mountains. It was not easy. It was very hot. We worked and lived side by side with the Cubans, most of them regular labourers, a few volunteers from urban areas, a few students from other countries. The menu at the camp was basic: fruits and vegetables, sausages, nothing fancy, not large rations, but enough to work on. At night we socialized and tried to get enough sleep to prepare us for the next day's exertions.

By the fourth week we had reached Santiago, Cuba's second largest city, in the eastern part of the island. We arrived in time for a traditional street carnival that coincided with the anniversary of the Fidel-led insurgent attack on the Moncada police barracks, a national holiday celebrated as the beginning of the Cuban Revolution. The carnival activity in the streets was intense, with dancers and musicians everywhere, everyone in crazy costumes.

We were staying with the other international students in the residences at the University of Santiago. One morning a jeep roared into the plaza beside the cafeteria. Something was happening. I grabbed my camera. We all crowded around. Fidel's younger brother Raúl Castro was driving, and Fidel was standing up shouting a welcome to us. Then, in English, he said: "I understand there are some North Americans here, and I understand that North Americans think they can play baseball. Well! I challenge you to a game!"

Later that day a combined team of Canadians and Americans were playing baseball. The opposition was the regular University of Santiago team with Raúl Castro inserted at second base and Fidel pitching. I was catching for the North American team.

The Cubans, of course, were much better players, and by the second inning they were far ahead. To even things up, the teams switched pitchers, with Fidel coming over to our team, and our pitcher going over to them. For the rest of the game I caught Fidel. I had not worn catcher's equipment for a few years, but I held my mitt up there in the right place and

"I always thought I'd be fired for my beliefs, not my incompetence."

managed to hang on to whatever Fidel threw at me. He did not have excessive speed, but he had plenty of control. His curve broke with an amazing hook, and his knuckleball came in deceptively slow. However, he paid no attention to my signals.

At one point I called *time* and went out to the mound to confer. I thought for sure that someone would snap our picture as I stood there in my dusty catcher's outfit, glove in one hand, mask in the other, while Fidel told me, quietly, "*Hoy, los signales no están importantes.*" Apparently he did not take direction from other people, not even from his catcher. And as far as I know, that photo, famous only in my imagination, was never snapped. Even so, with Fidel's help, our team managed to hold down the opposition to one or two more runs.

Near the end of the game Che Guevara put in an appearance. He stood there in his olive green fatigues, smoked a cigar, and watched. As an Argentinean, he was not such a committed baseball aficionado.

I had once seen a CBC television documentary on Cuba that featured Che extolling the theory and practice of voluntary labour. The camera had caught him standing amidst the high cane, machete in hand, answering the interview questions in halting English. Che had defined Socialism as the abolition of the exploitation of one person by another.

That had made a lot of sense to me. I too was ready to swing a machete in the tropical sun to further such ideals. In fact, that was the reason I had applied to come on this student work visit to Cuba. I had not guessed that Che would be standing over by the dugout watching me play baseball with his pal, Fidel.

The night before the game I had been in the bleachers of this same stadium watching the Cuban National Ballet performing *Coppélia*. The day after the game I would listen to Fidel make an impassioned four-hour speech to a throng of almost a million people standing and cheering in the 98 degree sun. At the end, we would all link arms and sing *The Internationale*.

A few years after that game in Cuba, I was back in Vancouver playing ball with George Bowering on the infamous Granville Grange Zephyrs, scourge of the Kosmic League. But that is a tale for another day.

[2005]

On Labels

—✎ JANE RULE

*"I came out as a lesbian long
before I came out as a writer."*

■ Jane Rule did not like labels. Though she made her living by writing, the
name "writer" was the last by which she felt she could call herself, and that
society would call her. Otherwise known (sometimes incorrectly) as girl,
woman, lesbian, teacher, pornographer, Canadian, American and more,
Rule pushed back against society's instinct to categorize individuals.

FROM THE TIME WE are very young children we are taught to label
ourselves and other people in a variety of ways. But what begins as simple
information soon becomes more complicated, coloured by value judgments which are not always fixed or easy to understand. I was five before
I learned that being a girl had serious drawbacks, six before I discovered
that being left-handed was unacceptable, nineteen and travelling in Europe
for the first time before I had to apologize for being an American. Some
labels we can choose like a favourite hat; some we are simply stuck with
like a necessary cane. Those we outgrow, like "child," are replaced by "old
woman." Others we are comfortable with only after they really apply, as
I am now with the label, "writer."

By the time I was fifteen, I was sure I wanted to be a writer, and I wasn't shy of saying so. What kind of a writer, I wasn't yet sure. I was writing a lot of bad poetry, strongly metered and rhymed in imitation of Edna St. Vincent Millay and Eleanor Wylie, inspired for subject matter even by such heavy worthies as Milton. When my mother read my tragically touching, thumpingly rhymed poem on my own blindness, she laughed and saved the world from the bad poet I might have grown up to be. I retreated for a time to personal essays intended to amuse, and my mother, for whom laughter was the highest goal, approved. By the time I reached college at sixteen, away from my mother's comic influence, I began to write bad short stories in imitation of Katherine Anne Porter and Eudora Welty, heavy in symbolism and grotesque characters. One featured a black man with yellow hair and green eyes, named Cain, who raped sheep. That story inspired my classmates to burst into the Wiffenpoof song — "We are little black sheep who have gone astray, bah, bah, bah" — every time they saw me.

Tough critics like my mother and my classmates daunted me a little.

Then I learned that in academic circles a real writer was by definition dead. Those foolish enough to be alive were not real writers at all, but "creative" writers, a swell-headed, deluded lot with nothing important to say. That attitude taught me if not real modesty some caution about exposing my ambitions. I gradually learned not to call myself a writer at all. As a young university teacher, I did not admit that what I did in my spare time was write short stories and novels. During the ten years I wrote before I had any publishing success, writing was a secret vice to be confessed only to intimate friends.

A few years ago the Canadian Writers' Union was concerned about how few young writers were applying for membership and tried to think of ways to make them more welcome. I pointed out that it was, in fact, very difficult to admit to being a writer. Only years of experience which tended to thicken the skin made such a confession possible. In my personal world I came out as a lesbian long before I came out as a writer. The Union should be resigned to being an organization for the middle-aged and the old.

I finished my third novel, which would be my first to be published, a few days before my thirtieth birthday. It took three years to find a publisher. I don't know what I expected beyond finally feeling I might have a legitimate claim to call myself a writer, or, if not anything as grand on the slim proof of one published book (anyone can write one book), at least permitted to say that I wrote. Instead in 1964, before homosexual relationships were removed from the criminal code, I became Canada's only visible lesbian and almost lost my job at UBC. I was defended by my colleagues with the old saw, "Writers of murder mysteries are not necessarily murderers." To my interviewers I was not a writer but a sexual deviant.

Years later my good friend, Don Bailey, told me that in all his years of publishing poems and stories and novels, no interviewer ever wanted him to talk about his writing, which he began in jail serving a term as a bank robber. They wanted him to talk about robbing banks. Over a bottle of scotch, we decided we should have a TV program called "The Lesbian and the Bank Robber" and give the public what they apparently want.

José Saramago, in his novel *Blindness*, says that if we first contemplated all the possible ramifications of our words or actions, we would be struck dumb and freeze. We can't possibly know and therefore take responsibility for the effect our words may have on others. As Auden says in "In Memory of W.B. Yeats," poetry is "modified in the guts of the living." Certainly Goethe, when he wrote *The Sorrows of Young Werther* didn't intend or expect to inspire a rash of suicides all across Europe. Yet we are often expected, like parents, to take responsibility for what our work, however distorted and misrepresented, does out in the world.

I am also labelled a pornographer because my books, coming from the States where some stay longer in print than they have in Canada, are routinely seized at the border by Customs, but none has finally ever been refused entry. Still the label sticks, and readers who buy my books are therefore often disappointed, and others who might otherwise buy and enjoy them don't.

I have done relatively little to publicize my work, weary of the roles I've been forced to play, but, when I agree to be interviewed, I give up any notion of speaking as a writer and become instead a teacher about gay issues, about censorship, about civil liberties, a responsibility I take seriously, not so much as a writer but as a citizen.

My first published novel came out just before I became a Canadian citizen. It is a book set in the States, probably accurately called an American novel. I have since been challenged about what right I have to call myself a Canadian writer, even though the majority of my fiction has been set in Canada. My Dutch publisher, arranging a publication party for one of my novels, approached the Canadian Embassy for a small contribution, only to be told that I was really an American. "Odd," replied my publisher, "since another branch of your government contributed funds for translating the book." I have been told that some Canadian writers travelling abroad are pleased to be mistaken for American and therefore part of a larger and more established and respected tradition. Only strong nationalists like Margaret Atwood insist on being identified as Canadian and become ambassadors for Canadian literature. For immigrants (another possible label) it is often difficult to know what use there is or what right we have to claim our citizenship as part of our identity. I felt guilty the first time I travelled in Europe with a Canadian passport and enjoyed the courtesy and kindness so often withheld from Americans, for under-

neath that bland label lurked surely still an ugly American. I should probably have been called an ex-American writer. Even now, after fifty years
in this country and very proud and relieved to be a Canadian, I am shy to
claim the label and never surprised if others are reluctant to grant it.

Because only a very few fiction writers or poets make even a modest
living from those activities, many turn to other forms of writing to pay
the rent. Betty Jane Wylie, a playwright and poet, as well as a wife and
mother of four children, was widowed suddenly in her forties and faced
the task of not only raising four children alone but supporting them as
well. She was amazingly successful, writing books of advice for widows,
cook books, writers' guide books, travel books, while she also occasionally took time to write a poem or play. Recently she was awarded the
Order of Canada. An interviewer, seeing listed among her many accom-
plishments a book on using leftovers, wanted her advice on how to use
up what was in his refrigerator. She snapped back, "I don't suppose I was
given the Order of Canada because I know how to clean out your fridge."
Genre labels make most writers uncomfortable in a culture that rates
writing narrowly and strictly to exclude or at least place below the salt
how-to books or children's books or mysteries or science fiction as not
really literature. Even best sellers and women's fiction are suspect. A poet
isn't a real poet if he or she is funny or sings poems to a guitar accompani-
ment. Genre labels are not meant to be descriptive so much as judgmental.
Real writers don't write cook books or jokes or murder mysteries. Real
writers die of starvation years before they can reap the rewards of their
immortal words. And their names are often "anon."

Although some claim that "anon" was a woman, gender labelling of
writers has been a long debate. Many women writers in the past chose to
avoid the label with masculine pen names, and that still is the habit of
many mystery and science fiction writers who fear otherwise putting off
their male readers. One bookseller I know makes a habit of misleading
men into buying women's writing so disguised. Until the present women's
movement made many women rethink their attitudes toward themselves
as women, even writers who didn't disguise their gender often refused to
be included in women's anthologies or published in women's magazines,
not wanting to be ghettoized.

Certainly some gay writers resist the label, not now so much in fear of criminal charges or job loss or alienation from family but of being placed in an even smaller ghetto, cut off from the main stream of literature, from larger audiences of readers.

Disguised or denied sexual identity rarely works. The first novel of James Baldwin's I read was *Giovanni's Room*, a story of two white male homosexuals in France. I didn't know he was black until I read others of his books, less self-conscious and much more powerful when he wasn't hiding his race or his sexuality in white characters. Who we really are nourishes what we write, and energy is better spent transcending than denying limiting labels. That choice also has the virtue of inspiring great loyalty in core audiences, ethnic, racial, sexual, who will be there for us even if the cross-over audiences publishers are always wooing don't happen to cross.

If we could be identified as many-labelled, which all of us are, we might move more comfortably in the world. Even if we could wear only those labels appropriate for the occasion, much as we select among our shirts or rings, we would be less apt to be embarrassed and irritable.

Auden said, "I am a poet only when I'm writing a poem." Because writers so often feel they may possibly never write another worthwhile word, putting down the label except while involved in the activity can be an enormous relief. For a long time I wanted to be even freer than that. I didn't want to be a writer at all. I simply wanted to write, and being a writer got in the way of that because what the world wants of a writer is not writing but public performing, lectures, readings, seminars, for which we are often paid more than we are for the writing we do. Now that I am retired, I write only very occasionally as I have this small essay, which seems like a grandchild come to visit for a few days. I don't find it as difficult to "be a writer." But the old are forgetful of nouns. Proper nouns go first, then common nouns. They are, after all, the only words we have to teach children who learn other parts of speech, even verbs and their tenses, by themselves. We are not finally labellers. The real business of our lives is to live, to love, to write, and to remember to leave the calling of names to others, names we may answer to or not.

[2005]

The Heterosexual Cage of Coupledom

﹁ JANE RULE

■ Jane "Jinx" Rule, who died with her typical dignity in 2007, was one of
the most mature, humorous and responsible voices in Canadian letters,
as well as an articulate spokeswoman on issues pertaining to personal
liberty and social responsibility. The following essay is Jane Rule's surprising
response to Canadian legislation that legally ensconced homosexual
common-law partnerships as equivalent to heterosexual common-law
partnerships in terms of rights and responsibilities. Rule critiques the
legislation as "neither the right to marry nor the right to remain private
and independent in our relationships."

OVER THIRTY YEARS AGO, when homosexual acts between consenting
adults were decriminalized, Trudeau said that the government had no
business in the bedrooms of the nation. Until a few months ago that privacy was respected.

Now the government has passed a law including gay and lesbian couples
as common-law partners with the same rights and responsibilities as
heterosexual common-law partners. Any of us who have lived together

in a sexual relationship for over two years must declare ourselves on our income tax forms, or we are breaking the law.

With one stroke of the pen all gay and lesbian couples in Canada have been either outed if they declare or recriminalized if they do not. Our bedroom doors have come off their legal hinges.

Why then is there such support for this new law among gay people? Svend Robinson spoke in favour of it in the House. EGALE, the national organization for gays and lesbians, encouraged its passing.

It is celebrated by all of them as a step along the road to total social acceptance, to a day when those of us who wish to can be legally married, our relationships just as respectable as those of heterosexuals.

But common-law partnerships were never about respectability. They were forced on couples as a way of protecting women and children from men who, by refusing to marry, were trying to avoid responsibility, free to move on when they felt like it without legal burdens of alimony and child support, without claims on their property or pensions.

There are some gay and lesbian couples raising children who, because they are not allowed to marry, may find a common-law partnership useful for benefits in tax relief, health benefits, pensions, if they can afford to expose themselves to the homophobia still rampant in this country. The law may also protect those who are financially dependent on their partners from being cast aside without financial aid.

But the law, far from conferring respectability, simply forces financial responsibility on those perceived to be irresponsible without it. What

about those poor who are unable to work because they are single parents or ill or disabled?

The single mother on welfare has long had her privacy invaded by social workers looking for live-in men who should be expected to support her and another man's children. Now single mothers must beware of live-in women as well. The ill and disabled will also be forced to live alone or sacrifice their benefits if their partners have work. With all that we have learned, we should be helping our heterosexual brothers and sisters out of their state-defined prisons, not volunteering to join them there.

Over the years when we have been left to live lawless, a great many of us have learned to take responsibility for ourselves and each other, for richer or poorer, in sickness and in health, not bound by the marriage service or model but on singularities and groupings of our own invention. To be forced back into the heterosexual cage of coupledom is not a step forward but a step back into state-imposed definitions of relationship.

We should all accept responsibility for those who must be dependent — children, the old, the ill and the disabled — by assuring that our tax dollars are spent for their care. We should not have any part in supporting laws which promote unequal relationships between adults, unnecessary dependencies, false positions of power.

No responsible citizen should allow the state to privatize the welfare of those in need, to make them victims to the abilities and whims of their "legal" keepers. Human rights are the core responsibility of the government.

The regulation of adult human relationships is not.

To trade our freedom to invent our own lives for state-imposed coupledom does not make us any more respectable in the eyes of those who enjoy passing judgment. We become instead children clambering for rule, for consequences to be imposed on us instead of self-respecting, self-defining adults.

Those of us who want to legalize our relationships for the protection of our children, for our own security, for whatever reason, should have the right to do so but not at the expense of imposing that condition on all the rest of us.

What we have now is neither the right to marry nor the right to remain private and independent in our relationships. What kind of victory is that?

[2001]

The Narrowness
of Vladimir Nabokov

_⌐ STEPHEN VIZINCZEY

■ A columnist for _BC BookWorld_ in its early years, Hungarian-born Stephen Vizinczey is a Canadian citizen who lives in London and Italy. Brilliant, highly opinionated and still going strong at eighty, the iconoclastic Vizinczey has written one of the best-selling Canadian novels of all time internationally, _In Praise of Older Women_, as well as _An Innocent Millionaire_ and _Lies in Literature_. Here he reviews _Vladimir Nabokov: Selected Letters 1940–1977_ edited by Dmitri Nabokov and Matthew J. Bruccoli (Weidenfeld and Nicolson).

"DIP IN ANYWHERE, and delight follows," John Updike assures us on the jacket flap of this 565-page volume.

Don't you believe it.

If you dip in anywhere you are likely to find yourself reading a business letter to a publisher agent, university president or the head of a foundation, museum or library. There are far too many of them, and all they tell you is that a writer has to write a lot of letters to make a living. Letters on lepidoptera and chess do not relieve the tedium. Dmitri Nabokov imposes on the reader when he claims that this collection reflects his father's "evolution as a writer and insights into his creative process."

If the intention was to reflect Nabokov's evolution as a writer, the most important letters would be the early ones, from his childhood and youth, but they are not here. The best part of the book contains the letters to his family, the only ones with recognizable human content that gives us some notion of Nabokov as a human being. But again, there are too few of them. . . .

The book was compiled for an American publisher and was clearly intended for the American academic market, which devours trivia about writers and literature as a way of distancing incompetent professors from literature itself.

The general reader in the UK where I live (assuming that there is a general reader) would be well advised simply to scan the index and look up the names that interest him or her. Some, of course, leap out of the lists. For example, Lyndon Johnson was the recipient of a telegram: "Wishing you a perfect recovery and a speedy return to the admirable work you are accomplishing." The date is 9 October 1965, the second year of the Amer-

The guy who writes
dust jacket blurbs.

ican involvement in the Vietnam War. This does throw some light, I think, on Nabokov's rather primitive understanding of politics.

America's misguided war in Vietnam was the greatest book to Communists: it cast them in the role defending national and Asian independence; and indeed Communism has been dying ever since the war's disastrous effects subsided. This was clearly seen by many people even at the time, but Nabokov's political understanding was on the level of slogans, which of course did not prevent him from pontificating on such matters with the greatest hauteur. "Your articles in the *Herald Tribune* counteract wonderfully the evil and trash of its general politics," he wrote to William F. Buckley, Jr.

From a letter to the editor of the *Daily Telegraph* magazine we learn that Nabokov did not enjoy music: "Dear Sir, I have received your kind letter offering me to interview Mr. Stravinsky in Marrakesh. I'm afraid there must be some misunderstanding. I hardly know him. I do not care for music in any form. I never interview anybody anywhere."

There is a witty letter to the *Sunday Telegraph*: "Sir, I cannot resist correcting a cruel misprint in your caption under the photograph of King George V, Tsar Nicolas II, and his son, the Tsarevich. The inadvertent substitution of "Tovarich" for the last word is especially distressing in view of the fact that it was indeed a *tovarisch* ('comrade' in the Bolshevist sense) who was a few years later to murder the poor little boy."

Nabokov wrote eloquently to *The Observer* in support of Vladimir Bukovsky, who had been transferred to a labour camp after "five years of martyrdom in a despicable psychiatric jail." However, in a 1968 letter written for him by his wife Vera, he is decidedly less generous to Marina Tsvetaeva, who lost her husband and daughter to the Stalinist terror and hanged herself in a provincial town where she couldn't even get work as a laundress:

"We wonder if you realize that although Tsvetaeva was living in a great poverty she was not much worse off than most writers. Tsvetaeva was published more than most other poets, even by those who did not much care for her as a person. Her complaints are very . . . exaggerated. . . . In her letters there is a constantly recurring whining note which is not exactly endearing."

All in all, it is not easy to find that "basically reasonable and decent man" of whom Updike speaks on the jacket. In these pages Thomas Mann is "plodding and garrulous," Sartre and Bertrand Russell are writers "with whom I would not consent to participate in any festival whatever," Edmund Wilson is an "ignoramus," Saul Bellow is "a miserable mediocrity," Sitwell is a "ridiculous mediocrity."

Doctor Zhivago, which came out around the same time as *Lolita* and competed with it on the best-seller lists, drove Nabokov into paroxysms of jealous rage. I'm not an uncritical admirer of *Doctor Zhivago* but still, calling it "that trashy, melodramatic, false and inept book . . . a sorry thing, clumsy . . . with stock situations and trite characters . . . corpselike . . . false and completely anti-liberal" is a bit thick.

However, Updike, whose review of *The Defence* Nabokov described as "charming, intelligent, witty and splendidly phrased," is much admired: "Dear Mr. Updike, I was delighted to receive your charming note. As you know, I love your prose. . . ."

Insofar as these letters really throw light on Nabokov, they help to explain the narrow range of his books. His obsession with literature as artifice, his immersion in the literary and academic worlds and his passion for such non-human pursuits as butterfly-collecting, did not help the novelist. Had he been less of a model family man and teacher, his fiction would have been richer. He lacked the large and often destructive appetites which make most great novelists. Would we have the same Dostoevsky without his involvement in conspiracy and his passion for gambling? Would we have Tolstoy without his drinking, gambling, religious mania and longing to remake Russia? Would we have Balzac without his monstrous acquisitiveness?

Let me draw your attention to a far better book in the same genre: *To the Happy Few: Selected Letters of Stendhal*, reissued not too long ago by the Soho Book Company, with Cyril Connolly's old but unsurpassable introduction. Stendhal had not only genius but an adventurous life fraught with danger and misfortune. "You can read your way out of anything with this," wrote Connolly. "It is another world and a better one."

That is true.

[1990]

The Conqueror & the Concubine

⟿ A.T.

■ Amanda Hale's novel *The Reddening Path* (Thistledown) is the story of a Guatemalan adoptee, Paméla, raised in Toronto, who returns to Guatemala to search for her Mayan birth mother. Concurrently, Hale re-imagines the love affair between the Spanish conqueror Hernán Cortés and his indigenous translator and concubine, Malinche. The resourceful Malinche learned Spanish, became Cortés' mistress, enabled him to overcome Montezuma and bore him a son named Martín. To this day, the derogatory word *malinchista* is used by Mexicans to describe someone who unduly apes the language and customs of another country. The appearance of *The Reddening Path* prompted this essay/review to consider Malinche as one of the more remarkable and influential women in North American history.

TO APPRECIATE THE LIFE story of Malinche, it's necessary to revisit the year 1511 when Diego Velázquez was sent from Hispaniola to conquer and explore Cuba. He brought along an ambitious young secretary, Hernán Cortés, who became the first mayor of Cuba's second largest city, Santiago de Cuba, on the eastern end of the island.

Charming and well-educated, Cortés was also untrustworthy. At age thirty-four, having jilted a Spanish noblewoman and upset Governor Velázquez, he hurriedly sailed from eastern Cuba for the Mexican mainland in 1519, eager for riches. With 508 soldiers, plus about 100 sailors, Cortés easily overcame some coastal Indians at Tabasco. They had never seen horses before and initially thought a man on a horse was a single beast.

A truce was arranged on March 27, 1519. Defeated chiefs in the Tabasco area brought Cortés gold, food and twenty female slaves. Among these "cooks" was a sixteen-year-old woman who spoke the local dialect, as well as the Nahuatl language of the much-despised Aztecs who occupied the interior of Mexico. Evidently high-born by virtue of her intelligence and bearing, she was christened Doña Marina. It wouldn't do to have sex with an infidel.

Cortés initially gave this unusual woman to his close friend, Alonso Hernández Portocarrero, but when it soon became apparent Marina could be extremely useful for his expedition — and she was beautiful in the bargain — Cortés conveniently sent Portocarrero to deliver an update on his success to King Carlos V in Spain, thereby making it easy for him to keep Marina for his own purposes.

Also in Cortés' entourage was a previously shipwrecked Spanish priest named Aguilar who could translate between Spanish and the local dialect. With the help of the Spanish priest, Marina's background became clear. She was the daughter of a Nahuatal nobleman or *cacique*, meaning chieftain. She had been sold into slavery by her mother after her father's death. Marina's mother had wanted to ensure her son from a second marriage would gain ascendancy.

A foot soldier with Cortés, Bernal Díaz, described Marina as "good looking and intelligent and without embarrassment." She was "a *cacica* with towns and vassals," and she learned Spanish quickly. Doña Marina soon became indispensable to Cortés as his translator and constant companion. Without her, a contingent of 1,300 Spaniards and Indians could never have defeated the Aztec empire.

To her own people, Marina would forever be known as *La Malinche*, meaning betrayer.

Continuing further west, Cortés established a settlement called Vera Cruz, not far from present-day Veracruz, where he learned of an enormous inland city, Tenochtitlán, on the site of present-day Mexico City.

At Vera Cruz, Cortés also first learned about the Aztec emperor, Montezuma II, who was represented by Teudilli of Quintaluor. When the explorer learned about Montezuma's magnificent inland city of Tenochtitlán (Cortés called it Temixtitlan — now it's Mexico City), he burned some of his own ships to prevent his men from turning back and informing Cuba's Governor Velázquez of his plans.

The Aztecs were a nomadic civilization that had migrated from western Mexico to the valley of Mexico during the fourteenth century, supplanting the Toltecs. As luck had it for Cortés, the Aztecs were anticipating the return of their ancient feathered serpent god, Quetzalcoatl, from the east. Bringing gifts of gold to Vera Cruz, the Aztec delegations wanted to know if the strange and powerful visitors were gods or mortals.

With essential assistance from Marina, Cortés was able to take advantage of the situation and pretend to represent their prodigal god. Quetzalcoatl was from the city of Tula, north of Tenochtitlán, formerly the seat of power for the Toltecs who had dominated Mesoamerica from 850 A.D. to 1200 A.D.

When the Aztecs, or *Mexicas*, replaced the Toltecs in the Valley of Mexico, Aztec rulers had taken the name of Quetzalcoatl. The god had deserted the people and became known as Kukulkan among the Maya.

When the emissaries for Montezuma asked if this strange, helmeted man with the floating houses could be Quetzalcoatl, Hernán Cortés — much like Sean Connery in the movie *The Man Who Would Be King* — wasn't about to disappoint. With the help of Marina, he did little to disabuse them of this notion. To this end, Cortés encouraged Indian suspicions that his men were immortal by burying his dead quickly. He also pretended to talk to his horse, as if his horses were rational creatures, like men.

Whereas the Aztecs had only seen chihuahuas, the Spanish had ferocious attack dogs. Armed with crossbows and *arquebuses* (Spanish muskets), and escorted by a dozen cavalry, the Spaniards overwhelmed and formed an alliance with the fearsome Tlaxcalan Indians near the coast, enemies of the Aztecs.

While on the coast, Marina infiltrated the local people and learned from an elderly woman that the Aztecs were planning a surprise attack. The woman's husband was a Tlaxcalan captain who had received gifts from Montezuma II to encourage the ambush. Cortés was able to launch a pre-emptive attack in Cholula, close to present day Puebla, killing some three thousand Cholulans and sending the Aztecs fleeing back to Montezuma.

The foot soldier Díaz praised Marina for helping to spare them from the Aztec priests who were known to cut open captives' chests, sawing through the breastbone with an obsidian knife, then ripping out still-beating hearts. According to Díaz, Marina "possessed such manly valour that, although she had heard every day how the Indians were going to kill us and eat our flesh with chilli, and had seen us surrounded in the late battles, and knew that all of us were wounded and sick, yet [she] never allowed us to see any sign of fear in her, only a courage passing that of a woman."

The Tlaxcalans marched with Cortés into the magnificent Aztec capital of Tenochtitlán ("the place where men become gods") on November 8, 1519. They crossed Lake Texcoco on a "broad causeway running straight and level."

Cortés and his men were overwhelmed by the size and richness of the Aztec capital with its 250-foot Pyramid of the Sun. Tenochtitlán had been developed over centuries by various peoples from approximately 150 BC to 750 A.D. Some five hundred years after its builders had disappeared from the site, the Aztecs arrived to possess it. By 250 A.D. it had spread to include nine square miles; by 450 A.D. it was possibly the largest city in the world. It has been estimated the city had a population of some three hundred thousand in about sixty thousand dwellings amid floating gardens.

Presents were exchanged but tensions grew after two Spanish envoys were killed. Surrounded by thousands of Aztecs, Cortés famously seized Montezuma II as his hostage. It was an impasse worthy of a Hollywood thriller. Montezuma II offered bribes to Marina if she would forfeit her allegiance to Cortés. Marina wasn't dissuaded. Montezuma II was ninth in a succession of powerful Aztec caciques; he had been in power for eighteen years — longer than Marina had been alive — but Marina some-how managed the negotiations between the two powerful men.

Although the Aztecs numbered some twenty thousand, by seizing their leader, Cortés dealt them a psychological blow. Cortés' distant relation, Francisco Pizarro, would adopt the same manoeuvre when he treacher-ously took the Inca leader Atahualpa hostage in 1532, defeating thousands of Incas with only 168 Spaniards.

Back in Cuba, Velázquez was determined to bring Cortés to trial. When Cortés learned that Velázquez was sending an eighteen-ship expedition with 900 soldiers under Panfilo de Narvaez to capture him, he decided to leave his lieutenant Alvarado and only 140 men, setting off to surprise the Spaniards with only 260 men of his own, taking Marina with him to serve as his translator.

The surprise attack worked. Cortés co-opted much of the Spanish force and hastened back to Tenochtitlán where the Aztecs had rebelled against Alvarado. Back at Tenochtitlán, Cortés asked Montezuma II to quell

Lovers

growing unrest among the Aztecs. As in *The Man Who Would Be King*, Cortés never understood that a tribal council of Aztec priests actually held sway, guided by oracles. When Cortés ordered Montezuma II to appear in public, the crowd hurled stones. One rock hit the emperor. Montezuma died three days later.

The Aztecs drove the Spanish out of the city on June 30, 1520. Aztecs attacked from canoes on both sides of the causeway as the Spanish fled. Cortés was almost captured in the confusion. At the ensuing Battle of Otumba, he lost 860 men. He lost seventy-two more men at Tustepec while retreating to his allied city of Tlaxcala. Once again he was fortunate. An outbreak of smallpox, brought by his men, decimated the Aztec population. Cortés reorganized that summer, incorporating equipment and reinforcements from Vera Cruz, and laid siege to the Aztec capital once more.

On August 13, 1521, the new emperor, named Cuauhtemoc, was captured. Entering the city, Cortés found it in ruins "like some huge church-yard with the corpses disinterred, and the tombstones scattered about." Famine and smallpox had been more lethal than guns. Cortés began building the Aztec capital that would become the world's most populated city. This marked the onset of Mexico's 300-year colonial history, ending in 1821.

In 1522, Cortés' first wife arrived unbidden from Cuba. She died almost overnight, inexplicably. This didn't help Cortés' already notorious reputation. Velázquez was conspiring against the disobedient and ungrateful Cortés in court, charging Cortés with failure to remit the *quito*, one-fifth of the booty required for the king. Cortés returned to face these charges in Madrid and was exonerated. He was then named governor, captain-general and chief justice of New Spain by King Carlos V in 1523.

During the conquest, Marina bore Cortés a son named Martín. After Cortés' second Spanish wife also bore him a son named Martín, the Mestizo (mixed blood) Martín became like a servant for his fully Spanish half-brother. When they were both arrested for plotting against the Spanish crown, the younger Martín was spared; the Mestizo Martín was tortured.

In 1524, having conquered Mexico, Hernán Cortés learned Cristobal de Olid had proclaimed the independence of Spanish Honduras. To remove this upstart official, Cortés began a gruelling overland trek towards Spanish Honduras that ranks with Hannibal's journey over the Alps. Departing from Vera Cruz on the Mexican coast, he marched in a straight line towards Trujillo on the east coast of Central America, torturing and hanging Cuauhtemoc along the way, having become obsessed with the notion that somehow Cuauhtemoc was planning a revolt.

This *entrada* of about 140 soldiers and several thousand Indians had to traverse high mountains and dense jungles. While slashing his way through uncharted territory, Hernán Cortés would have passed through the southwest corner of present-day Belize, making them the first Europeans to enter Belize by land. Order was easily restored in Honduras in 1525. (Cortés once said it was more difficult contending with his own countrymen than fighting against the Aztecs.)

Several attempts by Cortés to return to Mexico by sea ended in shipwrecks. Becoming despondent, he began dressing in the black robes of a Dominican monk, issuing morose premonitions of his own death. He eventually returned by sea to Mexico, via Cuba, thereby encircling Belize. In 1526 he was relieved of his command in Mexico City by Ponce de León, who died of fever after only twenty days in office. His successor died after two months. Once more, sudden deaths did little to enhance Cortés' reputation.

While remaining in control of Mexico from 1530 to 1541, he argued with Don Antonio de Mendoza, the first viceroy of New Spain, about who had the right to explore and annex California. Cortés consolidated and expanded his domain by exploring Guatemala, Honduras, Baja California and the Pacific Coast, but like Columbus he would ultimately feel inadequately rewarded.

Cortés was given the royal run-around for three years when he was debt-ridden and needed to make a claim on the royal treasury. His authority gradually eroded and his reputation waned especially after his participation in the unsuccessful 1541 Spanish expedition against Algiers. He became known as a chronic complainant. Accused of murdering his first wife (he strangled her but the Spanish government opted not to declare him innocent or guilty), Cortés was also long suspected of murdering a Spanish envoy in 1526.

While attempting to return to Mexico, Cortés was stricken with dysentery in Seville and died there on December 2, 1547. His remains were brought back to Mexico City and interred within the walls of a chapel behind the Hospital de Jesús, one of the many hospitals he founded.

As for Marina, the translator, she travelled with Cortés on his trek into Honduras, via Belize, to Trujillo, during which she re-united with her mother and half-brother, supposedly forgiving them. It is possible Marina was originally from the Belize/Honduras area, a Mayan descendant, but most researchers suggest she was from Paynala, the Gulf region of Coatzacoalcos, near the Tehuantepec isthmus, in which case her native tongue was Popoluca.

Having married Spanish soldier Juan Jaramillo, she settled in the province of Nogales. Cortés gave the couple an estate 50 miles north of Mexico City, and also gave her land on the Gulf, in her homeland, so that she might return there to die. Although Cortés has long been vilified by Latin historians and artists, his treatment of Marina makes it clear that he was not merely a brutal character.

Marina had at least one other child, Fernando Gómez de Orosco y Figueroa, born in Tlzapan, who died nine years later. In Amanda Hale's novel, Marina also gives birth to a daughter. It is believed Marina died at a relatively young age, around 1530, but exactly where and when remains unknown.

Although Marina clearly played an important part in Cortés' life, in his letters to King Carlos V, he mentions her only twice; he refers to her as "my interpreter, who is an Indian woman" in the second, and mentions her name in the fifth.

[2007]

Ape Populations
in Decline Worldwide

BIRUTÉ MARY GALDIKAS

■ On the occasion of her publication of *Great Ape Odyssey* (2005), Biruté Galdikas, the world's foremost protector of orangutans and their habitat, provided the following essay for *BC BookWorld* to describe the alarming rate at which the natural habitats of great and small apes are being decimated, and the implications of humans losing their closest kin on the planet.

WHEN I FIRST STARTED studying orangutans in the great tropical rainforests of Indonesian Borneo (Kalimantan), all that science knew about these enigmatic red apes in the wild might have filled a page. That was almost thirty-five years ago. We now know much more about orangutans but, unfortunately, we also know that orangutan populations have declined precipitously over the last few decades and that 80 percent of orangutan habitat has been decimated.

Along with the African chimpanzees and gorillas, the Asian orangutans are great apes, our closest living relatives in the animal kingdom.

Chimpanzees are so closely related to humans that their genome differs by only 1.2 percent in terms of single nucleotide changes and, once blood types are matched, chimpanzees can receive blood transfusions from us and vice versa. Gorillas, the greatest of the great apes in terms of size, are also very closely related to humans who, in some ways, are just another African ape.

All great apes share with humans high cognitive abilities, similar emotions, foresight, excellent memories, self-recognition and self-awareness, and are capable of symbolic communication, insight, imitation and innovation as well as generalization, abstract thought and problem solving. When we look into their eyes, we see something there that we recognize. Their eyes reflect our own.

Less known are the small apes, gibbons and the siamang. After the great apes, the small apes are our closest living relatives. Found only in Southeast Asia and China, small apes are territorial, monogamous, and the acrobats of the primate world, swinging from tree to tree like the "daring young man on the flying trapeze" and then soaring mid-air as they let go of one branch and fly to reach another. Certainly, this soaring locomotion is their form of genius. Gibbons are also known for their soprano vocalizations. Gibbons don't use tools and don't perform well in laboratory tests, scoring below some monkeys on intelligence tests. But studies of their brain show cerebellums that fall on the great ape side of the divide. And I have personally seen one captive gibbon, to my amazement, use tools, twigs, to scratch himself. I think gibbons are underrated. They are as flighty, edgy, and fragile as the birds with which they share the treetops. But they are brighter, smarter and more adaptable than they have been given credit for in textbooks.

Unfortunately, all apes, great and small, are in dire straits. All face extinction as their habitats are destroyed. When I first arrived in Borneo over 90 percent of the island consisted of primary tropical rainforest, the world's second-largest continuous expanse of forest after the Amazon Basin.

But now Borneo's forest is in retreat, like the forests of equatorial Africa, under relentless pressure from the forces of the global economy. Like a high-speed locomotive with no one at the controls, the global economy hurtles recklessly into the future, overwhelming everything in its path, destroying habitats and accelerating the extinction of plants and animals as well as the destruction of traditional human communities that coexisted with and sheltered the ecosystems in which the apes lived.

The prognosis for all ape populations in the wild is bleak. As habitat loss continues, ape populations decline and fragment, creating smaller populations that are increasingly vulnerable to local extinction. Local extinctions are common. In the African nation of Togo, once 33 percent forest, the forest is now almost gone. Not surprisingly, the western chimpanzee recently went extinct in Togo. In Nigeria and Cameroon, the Cross River Gorilla has the lowest population of any African great ape, with only 150 to 200 left. In China, due to recent industrial development, the call of the Hainan gibbon can only be heard in captivity. On the island of Java the endemic gibbon is found in only two protected mountainous areas and numbers less than two thousand. In Sumatra the orangutan population is critically endangered; some populations number only in the dozens.

Jane Goodall has been on the road tirelessly since 1986 championing chimpanzee conservation and animal rights. Yet chimpanzee habitats are shrinking. In West and Central Africa, chimpanzees are just meat for the pot. Unless politicians, rock stars, and governments embrace the cause of great and small ape extinction in a major way, apes will go extinct within the next fifty years.

The one bright spot remains the mountain gorillas. Dian Fossey gave up her life in 1985 for the gorillas. The tourist industry that followed helped provide stability and money, allowing for a 17 percent increase in gorilla numbers since the last census. It costs $50 for a park ranger to guide you to the cabin where Dian lived and the grave where she lies buried. It costs $350 per day for one hour with the gorillas. The mountain gorillas are as expensive as some lawyers. That has been their salvation.

I'm not saying we need more martyrs to ensure the survival of the great and small apes, but the Hollywood movie *Gorillas in the Mist* sure helped. And International Orangutan Awareness Week also helps hold back the tide. It could be a lot worse. Orangutans could be extinct throughout their entire range and not just locally. We need a *Mission Impossible* like those led by Bono and Bill Gates in their fight against global poverty and disease. We need to pressure our governments to save the great and small apes. An occasional billionaire would help, too.

Why save the apes? I could give ecological and even economic answers but the truth is greater. The great and small apes represent who we once were and where we came from. They are not our ancestors but our siblings, brother and sister species, and our cousins. They led the way and we followed, eventually overtaking them as we became human, and then we left them behind. That separation should not be their death sentence. What consolation is solitude if we remain the only species in our family left behind on a planet endlessly spinning, with no close kin to call our own?

[2006]

Schweitzer's Angel

—⌐ A.T.

■ The trio of Jane Goodall, Dian Fossey and Biruté Galdikas are often
described as Leakey's Angels because all three women have pursued
groundbreaking studies of primates after meeting archaeologist Louis
Leakey. In the same manner, little-known Louise Jilek-Aall of Tsawwassen
could well be described as Albert Schweitzer's Angel.

AS A MEDICAL STUDENT in Oslo, Louise Jilek-Aall was deeply impressed when the Christian missionary Albert Schweitzer delivered his Nobel Peace Prize speech on November 4, 1954, at Oslo University. Schweitzer had been awarded the Nobel Prize in 1952 but his duties in Africa had prevented him from appearing at the award ceremony. Seven years later Jilek-Aall arrived unannounced at Schweitzer's jungle hospital in Lambaréné, Gabon.

"And what do you want to learn from me?" he asked.

She nervously blurted out, "I want to learn to extract teeth."

Schweitzer's work as a physician in Africa, from 1912 to 1965, has inspired Louise Jilek-Aall ever since. Today she keeps a grass mat tapestry hanging over her kitchen table that was given to her as a parting gift by Schweitzer, also a scientist/philosopher and music scholar. His famous clinic was the subject of her second book, *Working with Dr. Schweitzer: Sharing his Reverence for Life* (1990).

"In my work as a psychiatrist," she writes, "I am keenly interested in people who are role models and who serve as ego-ideals, especially for the young; but only a very few appear to be worthwhile models."

Before meeting Schweitzer, Louise Aall worked as a bush doctor in Tanganyika/Tanzania and received the Henri Dunant Medal from the Red Cross for distinguished service with UN forces during the Congo civil war in 1960. Revised and updated, Jilek-Aall's first book *Call Mama Doctor: Notes from Africa* (WestPro) is a superb collection of remarkable stories recalling her experiences in Tanganyika/Tanzania. The stories are both harrowing and touching — because she continuously took risks beyond the confines of an established clinic.

In Tanganyika, Jilek-Aall discovered outcasts in the Mahenge Mountains who suffered from a severe form of epilepsy, prompting her to create the Mahenge Epilepsy Clinic to treat patients and educate families about epilepsy and its modern treatment. Epilepsy sufferers in Mahenge are no longer stigmatized or forced to live as outcasts.

As well as having a medical degree in tropical medicine, Dr. Louise Jilek-Aall speaks Norwegian, English, German, French, Spanish, Swedish, Danish and Swahili. She and her husband Dr. Wolfgang G. Jilek are trans-cultural psychiatrists and anthropologists who have been members of the UBC Faculty of Medicine since 1975.

The Jilek-Aall family has continuously supported the Mahenge Clinic and initiated research into epilepsy with teams of specialists from Canada, Austria, Germany and Tanzania. They have scientifically confirmed the existence of a unique form of epilepsy ("head nodding syndrome"), first described by Dr. Aall in the 1960s.

She now works to confirm its likely source is a parasite found in many tropical regions (Filaria-worm *Onchocerca volvulus*).

Jilek-Aall's fascinating stories arise from the intersection of trans-cultural psychiatry, bush doctoring, folk medicine and groundbreaking scientific research.

Although *Call Mama Doctor* and *Working with Dr. Schweitzer* were also published in China, Japan and Hungary, Jilek-Aall's books are almost unknown in North America. In a nutshell, her first book was produced in order to shed light on the inspirational people of Tanganyika/Tanzania, and her second book sheds light on an inspirational character. Jilek-Aall has yet to write about her service with the UN and International Red Cross during the Congo civil war — and she has yet to write an extensive account of her main accomplishment: the Mahenge Clinic.

If the story of Dr. Jilek-Aall was ever made into a movie, it could begin when she returned to Europe from Africa determined to help solve the epilepsy problem in Mahenge. But where to start? "Epilepsy falls between the specialties of neurology and psychiatry," she writes. "It is a stepchild of medicine and therefore institutions for epileptics usually suffer from a lack of funds."

After she found work as a resident psychiatrist at the Zurich University Clinic, her lone supporter was Professor Manfred Bleuler, chief of psychiatry at the university clinic. He arranged for Jilek-Aall to present a briefing on her epilepsy treatment project to the man in charge of mental health initiatives at the World Health Organization's headquarters in Geneva.

The elderly man greeted Jilek-Aall from behind his dark glasses. He challenged her credibility from the outset. He wanted to know if she was a specialist in neurology. She stammered, and desperately tried to convince him to give her even a small amount of funding.

"Well then, young lady," he interrupted, and his voice sounded annoyed, "neither Professor Bleuler's recommendations nor your beautiful eyes will help you in this matter. Since there appears to be some virtue in your proposals, I suggest you come back to us when you are a specialist and you have made a name for yourself."

Initially crushed, she regained her self confidence. "I am going to build the treatment centre for kifafa even if I do not get any help from WHO!" she decided.

Bleuler arranged for her to work at the Swiss Institute for Epileptics in Zurich. "Whenever my clinic in Tanzania ran out of funds," she says, "I sent part of my salary to the nurse." Bleuler also contacted pharmaceutical companies to have them donate medications and funds for Mahenge.

Then Bleuler raised another hurdle for her to consider. Louise Aall was an attractive, vibrant young woman. Did she ever wish to marry? Raise a family? He cautioned her that devoting her life to Africa might require the sacrificing of her personal life. Clearly she was at a crossroads.

In Zurich, Jilek-Aall was contacted by a professor of pharmacology for whom she had brought some medicinal herbs from Africa. It turned out that bark she had received from a medicine man at Mahenge had anti-epileptic properties, as proven in a Swiss laboratory. A decoction of the bark had been administered to test rats and had indeed reduced the induced convulsions.

If Jilek-Aall would accept funding from the pharmaceutical laboratories, would she be willing and able to return to Mahenge in order to procure one thousand pounds of this bark for conclusive analysis?

"I was speechless," she writes. "It was as if suddenly all the patients in Africa came alive inside my head, rushing forward, laughing, crying, calling and demanding. To my surprise, my first feeling was apprehension rather than joy. Going to Africa right now? It would not be adventure any more — I knew that life too well. It was easy to dream about Africa in my comfortable apartment in Zurich — but to face all those problems again? What about my training which would have to be interrupted, and my well-paying job? I dropped my head in shame."

Perplexed about what to do with her life, Jilek-Aall was invited by an Austrian colleague at the clinic to accompany him for an afternoon drive. They had never met outside the hospital. He wanted to take some photographs of the lake. She agreed, but with little enthusiasm. As they drove along the lake, she was absent-minded, barely able to follow the conversation.

He set up his tripod. There was a marvellous view of an old castle. An amorous young couple was sitting on a bench. The Austrian proceeded to intrude upon their intimacy. The young man looked up with a frown and said something in Italian. Jilek-Aall's Austrian colleague responded with a joke in Italian. There was laughter. All was well. The couple said they did not mind being photographed with the castle in the background. The picturesque castle glowing in the setting sun was mirrored in the calm waters.

"And as I stood at the railing," Jilek-Aall recalls, "smiling to myself, a new awareness came over me. Never had the colours of the sky appeared so warm, the songs of the birds sounded so gay and the sight of gold-rimmed clouds filled me with such content. In my heart I recognized that it all happened because I was not alone."

On the drive back, she began to tell her colleague about Africa, about Mahenge. She also agreed to meet with the pharmaceutical representative to discuss the logistics of the proposal. Just as she was preparing to attend this meeting, her photographer colleague caught up with her. He asked if it would be of any help if he came along to Africa? "I have some experience in neurology and psychiatry," he said.

Jilek-Aall looked at this man with blank astonishment. It took her a moment to rearrange her thoughts. "Slowly a feeling of great relief spread through me," she recalls. "I would not have to go back to Africa alone." She realized she wanted to go to Africa with this man — and she still didn't even know his first name.

In 1963, Wolfgang Jilek — her Austrian colleague with the camera — and Louise Jilek-Aall came to Canada to attend McGill University to specialize in "trans-cultural" psychiatry. They mostly wanted to expand their horizons as doctors but the Canadian consulate advised them to arrive as immigrants.

Driving across Canada for a holiday, the couple was taken aback by the beauty of British Columbia. They discovered they could obtain positions at UBC, but only if they agreed to first work in an area that lacked psychiatrists. So they worked and thrived in the Fraser Valley, based in Chilliwack, from 1966 onward.

Relocation brought them into contact with members of different ethnic groups — specifically the Mennonites, Dutch Reformed Church members, Doukhobors and First Nations. As transcultural specialists, they were able to publish papers germane to their field of expertise.

Increasingly the couple provided psychiatric consultation to indigenous populations in the Fraser Valley and on the Pacific Northwest coast. Friendly visitors to their home have included the French anthropologist Claude Lévi-Strauss, Chief Jimmy Sewid of Alert Bay, Haida artist Bill Reid, Seshaht artist George Clutesi and the UBC anthropologist Wilson Duff.

They both received Masters degrees in anthropology from UBC. In 1970, Wolfgang Jilek founded the Canadian Psychiatric Association's Section on Native Peoples' Mental Health. His books include *Salish Indian Mental Health and Culture Change: Psychohygienic and Therapeutic Aspects of the Guardian Spirit Ceremonial* (1974) and a best-seller called *Indian Healing: Shamanic Ceremonialism in the Pacific Northwest Today* (1982).

Still vibrant at age eighty, Louise Jilek-Aall is now prepared to turn over management of the Mahenge Clinic to a younger generation. The rudimentary clinic has treated more than one thousand epilepsy patients and provided social support to their families, mostly from the Wapogoro tribe. For further information, consult www.MahengeEpilepsy.com

[2010]

Noam Chomsky and the New Military Humanism

—ᴄ TOM SHANDEL

■ Noam Chomsky has visited Vancouver on numerous occasions to speak. His lectures always attract large audiences in British Columbia. In 1988, filmmaker Tom Shandel interviewed Noam Chomsky in his office at MIT for his film, *America: Love It or Leave It*, on Vietnam war-resisters who came to Canada. At the time Chomsky was one of the pre-eminent critics of US policies in Vietnam. Here Tom Shandel offers recollections of Noam Chomsky and reviews Chomsky's book *The New Military Humanism: Lessons from Kosovo* (New Star, 1999), another Chomsky examination of how "thought control" works in the free world.

WHILE HIS NAME SEEMS ubiquitous, most people have only a fleeting impression that the tireless political polemicist Noam Chomksy also has something to do with linguistics. Born in 1928 and raised in New York's left-wing Jewish environment of the late Depression and the Second World War, Chomsky has no formal training in linguistics despite being a leading authority in his field. He once admitted he probably could not have gotten a teaching position in linguistics anywhere but MIT because as a science school, they care only about results.

The Massachusetts Institute of Technology has been happy with his results ever since 1957 when Chomsky published his groundbreaking *Syntactic Structures*. Following on many more linguistic offerings, this year he has published *New Horizons in the Study of Language and Mind* from Cambridge University Press. In Mark Achbar's companion book to the documentary on Chomsky, entitled *Manufacturing Consent*, MIT published an account of Chomsky's citations in scholarly works by others. Between 1980 and 1992, Chomsky had 3,874 citations in the Arts & Humanities Citation index.

The top ten resources were Marx, Lenin, Shakespeare, Aristotle, the Bible, Plato, Freud, Chomsky, Hegel and Cicero. From 1972 to 1992 he was cited 7,449 times in the Social Science Citation index, "likely the greatest number for a living person," and from '74 to '92 he was cited 1,619 times in the Science Citation index.

So Chomsky is, above all else, a hard worker. By 1993, his bibliography had over 700 entries. His more than seventy books range from *The Logical Structure of Linguistic Theory* to *Politics: American Power and the New Mandarins*. Most people think of him as a political commentator but it is Noam Chomsky's training in linguistics that has made him into a rigorous explorer of meanings behind the words.

Finding his office was not easy. MIT is across the Charles River from Boston. I remember rowing crews on the water and students throwing Frisbees on the wide lawns in front of a classical building with huge columns. All very patrician. I'm led behind the grand structures to an industrial-looking two-storey wooden building like the hangars that used to be at Jericho Beach or the old UBC wartime huts.

Up an outside metal staircase, in a plain hall, we come to an outer office staffed by a female secretary. Behind her is a rank of filing cabinets, back to back, probably about sixteen in all. These contain Chomsky's correspondence files. He is legendary for personally answering all his own mail, either by hand or by his own typing.

Going into his office, one finds a large poster of Bertrand Russell, the British mathematician, philosopher and anti-war activist, and clearly one of Chomsky's heroes. At the bottom is a Russell quote that surely has special meaning for Chomsky: "Three passions, simple but overwhelmingly strong, have governed my life: the longing for love, the search for knowledge and unbearable pity for the suffering of mankind."

Chomsky sits at his desk, covered in mounds of loose manuscripts, photocopies and newspaper cuttings. Chomsky is an ardent critic of the *New York Times*, the newspaper of record for America Inc. As his social sideline, Chomsky uses the *Times* to track the progress of US foreign policy. Bookcases surround him; an electric kettle sits steaming beside a teapot on a little table. The effect is a messy cave, the kind where only the owner knows exactly where everything is. I recall there was an old manual typewriter like George Woodcock's and probably George Orwell's. Yikes, I thought. Typing on a manual clunker.

My visit was to record his reflections on the Vietnam era and the "draft-dodgers" who fled to Canada. He swivelled around on his wooden office chair and launched into a lecture on Canada as an historical safety valve for American political tensions. He mentioned the underground railroad for the African American slaves before Emancipation, and the United Empire Loyalists leaving Boston for Canada in the 1800s. "That was nearly 4 percent of the entire population of the States that chose to leave the country for political reasons," he says.

Similarly, Chomsky says few Americans will acknowledge the roughly quarter-million young Americans who went to Canada in the Vietnam era because it doesn't fit the picture. And if it doesn't fit the picture, that young men and women would actually choose to leave America, then most Americans couldn't believe it if they heard of it.

Internet guy

Now, some thirteen years later, Chomsky hasn't changed his views of his country but he has incorporated some new opinions about the "new internationalism." Just as he monitored American delusions about Vietnam in the 1960s and East Timor in the 1980s, he has turned his critical attention to Kosovo in the 1990s for The New Military Humanism.

Chomsky is extremely critical of the military campaign in Kosovo. With his formidable intellect and scholarship he probes the events and illuminates the economic powers behind the screen the public sees. He discusses "the new humanism" of the "enlightened states" and he exposes their talent for "intentional ignorance" perpetrated in the name of globalization. This is a dangerous process he describes as "new colonialism."

Chomsky has gleaned all the records and sifted the lies, half truths and spins in government policy papers, scholarly work, the international press, and, of course, the *New York Times*. The Kosovo campaign was a crock, he says, poor in conception, with vague objectives and ineptly executed. This is what an inquiry by retired NATO Generals has just concluded. Now that the issue is no longer as contentious, the *New York Times* has reported the Generals' findings — but Chomsky was first off the mark.

"Intentional ignorance" is a characteristic of the "New Humanists" such as Tony Blair and Bill Clinton, especially when it comes to analyzing the consequences of actions. Whether it's Janet Reno in Waco, Texas, or the bombing blitzkrieg in Yugoslavia, the New Humanists carefully keep insulated from any moral responsibilities.

Chomsky illustrates how ethnic cleansing increased dramatically after the bombing started, as did "collateral" civilian deaths. So if America can intervene with the Serbs, why not address the plight of the Kurds in Iraq and Turkey? Chomsky explains the reasons.

As Chomsky said years ago, if it doesn't fit the picture, it can't be happening. What's good for General Motors is good for everybody. If you still need convincing about the crusade against Serbia, *Lessons from Kosovo* has more than fifty pages of notes and a proper index. Read it and your paranoia about the New World Order will be justified.

According to Chomsky, "the real drama since 1776 has been the relentless attack by the prosperous few upon the rights of the restless many."

New Star deserves a standing ovation for producing a significant book by an important international thinker about a troubling development in world governance and democracy. Other Chomsky titles from New Star are *Chronicles of Dissent* (1992) and *Class Warfare* (1997).

[2000]

Pitching *The Corporation* in Banff

JOEL BAKAN

In 1999, Joel Bakan attended the Banff Television Festival with Mark Achbar, one of the makers of *Manufacturing Consent: Noam Chomsky and the Media*, to propose a new documentary series about the history and nature of large corporations. From his perspective as a neophyte in Television Land, here is Joel Bakan's report on pitching *The Corporation* to television executives. The film *The Corporation* was released in 2003 and has been shown around the world.

PITCHING *THE CORPORATION* often seemed futile. After two days and a dozen pitches, I felt like Sanchos, with Achbar playing Don Quixote, tilting at satellite dishes. During each pitch we had to convince a distracted and overbooked broadcaster representative that our show was more exciting than all the others she or he had been pitched about. The problem for me, as an academic non-fiction author, was that most television people don't get turned on by ideas and analysis. Even the documentary side of television often seemed to be driven by entertainment concerns, with ideas taking a back seat or having to stand in the aisle. "That sounds like a great book idea," was a typical response. "But who are the characters?

What are the stories? Where's the drama?" I quickly learned to adjust the pitch, trotting out interesting stories and characters first, and then, slipping in an idea, an analysis, maybe even a statistic, as though it were an afterthought . The academic in me bristled. But this was showbiz.

Some television people seemed almost hostile to thought. Accepting his award for Ally McBeal, David E. Kelly told the adoring crowd how unfair it was that people criticized him for the show's portrayal of women. "It's just a story about a woman," he complained. "It's not meant to say anything about what women are or should be." Semioticians be damned! During this event I saw the back of Michelle Pfeiffer's head. In one session a big wig American producer snorted that the key-note address of the Festival, a graceful and constructive critique of television delivered by Mark Kingwell — Canada's hippest intellectual — reminded him again why he abhorred intellectual analyses of TV. Such anti-intellectualism is a strong voice in TV land, but not the only one. Some pitch sessions — such as ours with TV Ontario, the National Film Board, Vision TV and BBC, to name a few — were thoroughly engaging. In them I met TV people who were deep thinkers, and more intellectual fun than most of my academic colleagues. Perhaps the greatest frustration for me as a writer in TV land was the apparent irrelevance of writing — at least when pitching. Achbar and I brought a twenty-five page treatment document to Banff, a model of concision. Few wanted to read it. "Get it down to two pages" was the straight-faced advice from one Canadian broadcaster heavy. That seemed generous compared to the high-brow BBC, which wanted only one page. Television people want to hear you, not read you.

There was a certain irony in pitching *The Corporation* at Banff. Banff, after all, is hyper-corporate. Corporate logos, corporate sponsorships, corporate people were all over the place. At one event, Michael MacMillan, head of Atlantis Alliance Inc., was treated like some kind of demigod, escorted to the stage by four Mounties (their appearance licensed by corporate rival, Disney) and a pipe — simply to receive an award. Many of the people I spoke with seemed concerned about television's increasing corporatization. Partly to blame, according to some of them, is the Canadian funding structure. Outside of the slashed and burned CBC, private sector corporations, driven primarily by their — and their advertisers' — bottom lines, decide what we see on TV, and make lots of money for showing it. Public agencies subsidize the system by providing taxpayer cash, and the use of the publicly owned air waves. To take one example of the absurdity of this system, Atlantis Alliance, touted as a Canadian private-sector success story, and the eleventh largest production house in the world after Time Warner, felt compelled to kill *Justice*, its flagship show for next season, when public money from Telefilm Canada did not materialize.

Despite its dependence on public subsidies, Canada's TV industry, along with the rest of the corporate media, gripes constantly about government's overbearing presence. Saltspring denizen Mort Ransen, who made the critically acclaimed film *Margaret's Museum*, told me a chilling tale about his own experience with the media's bias against anything public. Ransen got his start in film at the National Film Board, but eventually left to make his own films. After his departure from the NFB, a reporter asked him what it had been like working there. He spoke briefly of some of the frustrations, but then went on at length about what a great institution it was. The resulting story: "Ransen Criticizes the NFB." Twenty years later Ransen was again asked about the NFB, this time by a reporter from a major Canadian newspaper. He told the reporter about his previous experience, and said he did not again want to be misrepresented. The reporter told him point blank that if he were to write anything positive about the NFB, or any other public agency, it would not get printed. And if he persisted in such writing, he would be fired.

But it's not all gloom and doom in television land. The independent television artists I met are reason for a cautious optimism about television's future. These mainly young writers, directors and producers are creative and tenacious, intensely committed to making challenging and edgy TV. Despite all its warts, television is pretty tempting. When I finally got him to stop schmoozing and sit down, Vancouver's own Mark Leiren-Young (now living in Toronto) summed up television's lure: "Television is incredible fun — it combines the adrenaline of journalism with theatre, and it's mind-boggling to think of the audiences you can reach." But, he added, you can't be just a writer in television land. "Frustrating as it may be, if you want to write your own stuff, you have to declare yourself a 'writer-producer.'"

Some great projects were being pitched at Banff by BC filmmakers — a vegan docu-comedy cooking show, a historical documentary about a Chinese leper colony on one of the Gulf Islands, a humorous magazine show dealing with social issues and a sitcom about temp work. The team responsible for this latter one wore hard hats to their pitch sessions as "protection from falling interest" and cordoned off their sessions with yellow emergency tape. Even I — a mere tourist in TV land — was tempted to stay at Banff. I was transfixed by one session, titled "Two in a Room," a cross between the one-day, novel-writing contest and "Wheel of Fortune." Two executives, each representing a different broadcaster, one Canadian, one foreign, sit on a stage and negotiate criteria for an international coproduction in front of some 500 people. Once the criteria are set, audience members are given two days to write up and submit proposals. The winning proposal gets a $10,000 development deal and a shot at having the show produced. After much drama and suspense, the two executives agreed the show should be about music, related to youth, entertaining, interesting and highly visual. My idea was "Hoof Dreams," a documentary about the resurgence of tap dancing among African-American youth. I think I could have smoked the winning idea, "Piano Lessons," a film about the relationship of pianists to their pianos, but I never got around to writing up my proposal. I was too busy pitching.

[1999]

"One day we'll have a
logo of our own."

Joel Bakan, the Noam Chomsky of Kitsilano

⤙ LISA KERR

■ No book by a British Columbian has stirred as much critical debate as Joel Bakan's *The Corporation: The Pathological Pursuit of Profit and Power* (2004), the print version of a feature film that won the top documentary award at Robert Redford's Sundance Film Festival. Here Lisa Kerr, an associate Editor for *BC BookWorld*, reviews Bakan's work in relation to that of his contemporaries commenting on the same social and commercial ills.

DURING ANTI-APEC protests at UBC in 1997, a young law professor named Joel Bakan looked out his office window, grabbed his library card — to identify himself as a professor — and took his copy of the Constitution of Canada with him to monitor the Sgt. Pepper Spray demonstrations.

It proved to be a memorable day. The RCMP defined where protestors could respond. It was automatically impossible for leaders of China and Indonesia to witness the protestors, and vice versa. The mounting frustration of demonstrators as they tried to scale a fence made a strong impression on Bakan. Canadians protesting the presence of dictators in their own country were portrayed on the evening news as anti-social elements.

Having just begun to develop a film project with Tom Shandel and Mark Achbar, maker of *Manufacturing Consent* with Noam Chomsky, Bakan and Achbar roamed the campus with Achbar shooting proceedings with his video camera. That day became a turning point in their efforts to make *The Corporation*, the controversial documentary that has won the top documentary award at Robert Redford's Sundance Film Festival.

"Most students in mid-1990s North America were building investment portfolios, not social movements," writes Bakan in *The Corporation: The Pathological Pursuit of Profit and Power* (Penguin, 2004). "Yet here they were, thousands of them, braving pepper spray and police batons to fight for ideals. Even more unusual, the students were protesting against corporations — against their destruction of the environment, exploitation of workers, and abuses of human rights."

In the wake of that APEC demonstration at UBC, anti-globalization protests followed in Seattle, Prague and Geneva. Then Wall Street scandals — at Enron, WorldCom and Tyco — confirmed suspicions that large corporations were often corrupt and largely out of control.

Bakan and Achbar, later joined by Jennifer Abbot, proceeded to gather interviews with CEOs, activists and philosophers — including Noam Chomksy and Michael Moore. They canvassed opinions across the corporate divide, from the likes of Michael Walker, head of the arch-conservative Fraser Institute, to Nobel Prize-winning economist Milton Friedman; from Oscar Olivera, who organized people's protests to water privatization in Bolivia, to Ray Anderson, CEO of Interface, the world's largest carpet manufacturer.

Now the film version of *The Corporation* has played to sold-out audiences across Canada. It won audience awards at the Vancouver, Toronto and Sundance festivals, along with the Joris Ivens Special Jury award at Amsterdam — the most prestigious documentary film festival in the world. It opens in US and UK theatres in June.

Whereas Bakan's first book, called *Just Words: Constitutional Rights and*

Social Wrongs, was an academic work about the protection of free speech under the Canadian Charter of Rights and Freedoms, *The Corporation* is intended to be more provocative. As in the film, corporations are compared to Frankenstein, sharks and psychopaths.

To grab attention, Bakan has incorporated the work of Dr. Robert Hare, an expert on psychopathy, whose checklist to identify psychopathic behaviour is used around the world. By referencing that list, Bakan and Achbar have determined corporations are, by their nature, essentially psychopathic. They allege that corporations often exhibit a callous unconcern for the feelings of others, they lack the capacity to maintain enduring relationships, they often show a reckless disregard for the safety of others, they can be deceitful through repeated lying and conning others for profit, and they rarely have the capacity for guilt.

Bakan contends the legal structure of the corporation is to blame for bad behaviour in the corporate world. That is, when a business chooses to "incorporate," the people running the show get a benefit called "limited liability." It means a director of a corporation can't get sued for wrongs committed on the job, so long as they're done in the "best interests of the corporation." Those interests are defined, quite simply, as making profits for shareholders.

Bakan showcases the anti-social record of General Electric, a corporation with repeated environmental violations and hundreds of millions of dollars in fines. But even more telling is the example of Henry Ford. In 1916 the car maker learned an important lesson. He had decided to return some of his company's handsome profits to his workers, with the idea that they could use their higher wages to buy a Ford motorcar along with more wealthy Americans. Ford's major shareholders, John and Horace Dodge, took Ford to court for this socialist concept and Ford was summarily rebuked by the judge for forgetting that a corporation could not be run "for the merely incidental benefit of shareholders and for the primary purpose of benefiting others."

This case is still taught as an introduction to corporate law: students learn that it's illegal for a corporation to do anything but make money for shareholders. Hence causing environmental damage or violating workers' rights, can be justified in the interests of capitalism as a necessary part of doing business, particularly when profits can outweigh the costs of defending a lawsuit or paying a clean-up fine.

These days sophisticated marketing departments understand that people are disenchanted by companies that destroy the environment and exploit child workers. The resultant new phenomenon of the socially responsible corporation is central to Bakan's scrutiny. The likes of Kathie Lee Gifford and Puff Daddy have recently scrambled to press conferences to denounce their involvement with foreign sweatshops. Shell Oil currently has a series of television commercials portraying employees who look more like foreign aid workers than oil executives. The message about these bright and compassionate people is clear: "they don't fight the oil company, they are the oil company."

"There's a sense out there today that because corporations can be socially responsible," says Bakan, "they can regulate themselves, and we no longer need regulation from the government in the form of laws. There's a real pairing of deregulation on the one hand and the appearance of social responsibility on the other, and that's the point to which I object. It's fine if CEO guys and gals want to be decent, but corporate benevolence is not a replacement for legal standards that constrain what corporations can and should do."

Or, as Noam Chomsky has pointed out, "it is better to ask why we have tyranny than whether it can be benevolent."

The Enron scandal shows what can happen when legal standards are eroded. In Bakan's book, the Enron story isn't just about worthless stock and lost pensions. Bakan traces how Enron began as a pipeline company, but soon moved into the more lucrative energy trade business. In the 1990s, Enron officials led by former CEO Kenneth Lay focused on political lobbying efforts to deregulate the trading of energy futures. Bakan describes a remarkable process of political fumbles as Enron succeeded in getting rid of government supervision of its business, by way of the Commodity Future Modernization Act. Once that law was passed, Enron used its newfound freedom to begin manipulating the California energy market.

Over the next six months, there were 38 blackouts in California. "The company helped manufacture an artificial energy shortage that drove the price of electricity, and consequently its profits, sky high," says Bakan. Ultimately on December 7, 2000, millions of Californians were suddenly without power. California residents had to pay outrageous power bills for what power they could get. On June 19, 2001, the Federal Energy Regulatory Commission finally responded by imposing price controls on California's energy market. Enron was caught by surprise, left with billions of dollars of contracts worth way less than what they had paid. Enron filed for bankruptcy four months later.

Naomi Klein, author of *No Logo*, points out that modern-day activists protest in front of Nike Town instead of Parliament. Bakan maintains it's time to return to government, and that the answer lies in changing the laws that regulate corporations. He cites Franklin D. Roosevelt's Depression-era New Deal as the first package of regulatory reforms aimed at "curbing the powers and freedoms of corporations." That era came to an end with Ronald Reagan, and for the next twenty years the mantra of privatization and deregulation took over.

Since then, corporations have been vying with government to take over public services. Claims for greater "efficiency" abound, but the privatization of essential public services is riddled with problems. Bakan looks at the example of Edison Schools, a US business with 133 schools under its control. When Edison's stock price fell it cut back on staff — 600 students in each school would make up for it with one hour of office work per day. When its Philadelphia schools weren't making enough money, the company sold off textbooks, computers, supplies and musical instruments.

Michael Walker of the Fraser Institute has advocated for more private control of the planet and its resources on the theory that when you own something you take better care of it. "What about when the most profitable way to exercise your ownership might be to exploit your property?" Bakan asks. "Or when taking care of the things you own means causing harm to those around you?"

The guy who carried a copy of the Constitution of Canada into a public demonstration is not a radical. Bakan is a former Rhodes Scholar and law clerk to Chief Justice Brian Dickson of the Supreme Court of Canada. He doesn't advocate the destruction of the corporate structure, nor does he seek to vilify the businessmen and women who spend their working lives in the service of a profit-seeking enterprise. His work simply sheds light on the motives of corporations, in order to instigate public awareness about the need for regulated industries.

But the huge success of *The Corporation* — a three-hour documentary that has sold far more tickets than most Canadian movies — has put Bakan and Achbar into the spotlight, and spotlight has brought them some heat. The *Vancouver Sun*'s Katherine Monk was among those who criticized Bakan and Achbar for their acceptance speech at Sundance, a speech in which they noted moviegoers had voted for their film on a Coca-Cola-sponsored ballot. They thanked Coca-Cola, sponsors of their prize, for a taste of the future, when corporations sponsor everything, including elections.

Bakan thought the crowd at Sundance appreciated the irony of the situation, and they "took it in the spirit in which it was given, a bit of light-hearted ribbing from a couple of filmmakers who were standing there receiving an award for a film called *The Corporation* which was critical of the corporation in a context that was totally overwhelmed by corporate sponsors."

But some commentators have accused Bakan and Achbar of impudence. Such a response reaffirms to Bakan a major treatise in their film, and his book — soon to be published in the US and beyond. When corporations show their benevolent side, critical voices are expected to fall silent.

[2004]

British Columbiana

The Ancient Mariner for Real:
Juan de Fuca

—๑ A.T.

kd lang's overwrought version of Leonard Cohen's "Hallelujah" was all very well. And it was great to have our local spoken-word poet Shane Koyczan recite his paean to how nice we are as Canadians at the opening ceremonies for the 2010 Winter Olympics. But imagine the bewilderment of the world — as well as 99.9 percent of British Columbians — if Olympic organizers had commissioned the province's foremost maritime historian, Barry Gough, to conceive the opening ceremonies and tell the story of how modern British Columbian society began. A public address system narrator would begin with, "Once upon a time, in a café in Venice, in April, in 1596. . . ." It was there and then, in a place not yet called Italy, that the English correspondence of merchant Michael Lok first attributes the earliest visit to the shores of what we now call BC by a European mariner, as Barry Gough has neatly outlined in the opening chapter for his 15th book, *Juan de Fuca's Strait: Voyages in the Waterway of Forgotten Dreams* (Harbour 2012). That ancient mariner is now commonly known as Juan de Fuca.

ACCORDING TO WRITTEN, eyewitness accounts, the first European mariner to have reached BC waters was the Spaniard Juan Pérez in 1774, some four years before Captain James Cook famously set foot at Nootka Sound in 1778, accompanied by British crewmen that included George Vancouver and William Bligh. As Barry Gough now makes clear, however, there is ample evidence to assert that the first "European discoverer" of BC was actually a Greek explorer named Apostolos Valerianos, sailing for Spain under the name of Juan de Fuca.

In *Juan de Fuca's Strait*, Gough carefully relates how Juan de Fuca was an old man when he met an English dealer in fine fabrics, Michael Lok, in Venice, in 1596. Lok, who also spoke French, Spanish, Italian and Latin, was acutely aware that major seafaring nations were hoping to discover a "northwest passage" to the riches of the Orient.

Lok was therefore fascinated by Juan de Fuca's account of a voyage made "up the backside" of North America, in 1592. The transplanted Greek, from the island of Kefalonia — the largest of the Ionian Islands along the Adriatic Coast, a place "held in fee" by the city state of Venice, acquired in 1500 — provided Lok with a detailed verbal summary of a voyage as far north as the 48th parallel, at which point he entered a waterway (that now bears his name), which he called the Strait of Nova Spain.

Lok, as an English consul, excitedly sent this news to England. The Greek/Spanish mariner was offering his services to the Queen of England for £100 to help England discover the Northwest Passage. Specifically, Juan de Fuca agreed to serve as a pilot if England provided a ship of forty tons. A pilot in a Spanish vessel, as Gough explains, corresponded to a first mate on English and American ships, second in command.

But Juan de Fuca also wanted the English to provide compensation for goods stolen from him by Captain Cavendish in 1587 when, on a return voyage from the Philippines and China on the 700-ton Manila galleon *Santa Anna*, Juan de Fuca was overtaken by Cavendish who stole his cargo valued at some 60,000 ducats, near Cabo San Lucas, where Juan de Fuca was put ashore with food and handguns.

Unfortunately for the English, Juan de Fuca's request for restitution could not be resolved quickly. Juan de Fuca returned to Kefalonia but continued to communicate with Lok, using his native Greek. When Lok wrote to Juan de Fuca in Kefalonia in 1602 and no reply was received, the

Englishman presumed, perhaps correctly, that Juan de Fuca must have died.

The written evidence that Juan de Fuca was the first European to discover the strait between Vancouver Island and Washington State that bears his name is provided in a remarkable compilation of travel literature called *Hakluytus Posthumus* or *Purchas His Pilgrimes; Contayning a History of the World in Sea Voyages and Lande Travells, by Englishmen and Others* in 1625.

Maritime historian Samuel Purchas based his entry about Juan de Fuca on letters written by Michael Lok, who had written to the Lord Treasurer, to Sir Walter Raleigh and to Master Richard Hakluyt, asking them to send £100 to bring Juan de Fuca to England.

As recorded by Samuel Purchas, the Viceroy of Mexico had sent Juan de Fuca "with a small Caravela and a Pinnace, armed with Mariners only" along the coast of New Spain and California in 1592. He sailed "until he came to the Latitude of 47 degrees and there finding that the land trended North and North-East, with a broad Inlet of Sea, between 47 and 48 degrees of Latitude, he entered there into, sayling therein more than twentie days, and found that land trending still sometime North-West and North, and also East and South-Westward, and very much broader sea than was at the said entrance, and that he passed by divers Illands in that Sayling. And that at the entrance of this said Strait, there is on the North-West coast thereof, a great Hedland or Iland, with an exceedingly high Pinacle, or spired Rocke, like a piller thereupon. Also he said, that he went on the land in divers places, and that he saw some people on Land, clad in Beasts' skins; and that the Land is very fruitful and rich of Gold, Silver, Pearle, and other things, like Nova Spania. And also he said, that being entered thus farre into the said Strait, and being come into the North Sea already, and finding the Sea wide enough everywhere and to be about thirtie or fortie leagues wide in the mouth of the Straits, where he entered he thought he had now well discharged his office and done the things he was sent to do."

It is important to note that Juan de Fuca claimed the entranceway to the great inlet between 47° and 48° was marked by "an exceedingly high Pinacle, or spired Rocke, like a piller thereupon."

The coastal historian Captain John T. Walbran later corroborated this report in his *British Columbia Coast Names*. He wrote, "This is substantially correct; the island is Tatooche, and the spired rock, now known as De Fuca's pillar, 150 feet high, stands in solitary grandeur, a little off shore, about two miles southwards of Tatooche Island."

The first English mariner to recognize Juan de Fuca's strait was Captain Charles Barkley on the *Imperial Eagle* in 1787 — almost two centuries after Juan de Fuca's voyage. He consequently named Juan de Fuca Strait because it lay above the 47th parallel, where Lok's report of Juan de Fuca's exploration had designated it to be.

Frances Barkley's diary of her husband's 1787 voyage recorded the following perceptions: "The entrance appeared to be about four leagues in width, and remained about that width as far as the eye can see. Capt. Barkley at once recognized it as the long lost strait of Juan de Fuca, which Captain Cook had so emphatically stated did not exist."

In 1847, American historian Robert Greenhow published a history of Oregon and California in which he supplied a summary of Juan de Fuca's life based upon the English and Spanish translations of the correspondence between de Fuca and Lok. In 1854, another American historian named Alexander S. Taylor took up the narrative by asking the American consul in the Ionian Islands, A.S. York, to gather any and all material concerning Juan de Fuca and his family.

York provided information gleaned from *The Lives of Glorious Men of Cephalonia* written and published in Venice in October 1843 by Rev. Anthimos Mazarakis, a Kefalonian. The book had been translated into Italian by Tomazeo. Taylor published two articles in the September and October 1859 issues of *Hutchings' California Magazine* that recounted what he had gleaned about Juan de Fuca's life.

According to Taylor's research, the ancestors of John Phokas (Fucas) fled Constantinople in 1453 and found refuge in the Ionian Islands. One brother named Andronikos Phokas remained as the head of the Phokas family. Another brother Emmanuel Phokas was born in Constantinople in 1435 and departed in 1470 for Kefalonia. Juan de Fuca was one of four sons born to Emmanuel Phokas, also known as Phokas Valerianos to distinguish him from the Phokas family in Argostoli. Emmanuel Phokas settled in a valley in southwestern Kefalonia, at Elios. In that valley was situated the village of Valeriano, now vanished. Most of the island's buildings were destroyed by an earthquake in the early 1950s. A statue of Juan de Fuca has since been erected. The neighbouring island of Ithaki is the legendary home of Odysseus; Kefalonia boasts Apostolos Valerianos (Juan de Fuca).

Juan de Fuca's Strait: Voyages in the Waterway of Forgotten Dreams represents a synthesis of forty years of research by Barry Gough into maritime exploration of the West Coast. After capably recounting this tale of the ancient mariner, Gough proceeds to illuminate the voyages of mariners in his wake, such as James Cook, Manuel Quimper, José María Narváez, George Vancouver, Juan Francisco de la Bodega y Quadra and Dionisio Alcalá Galiano.

[2012]

Francis Drake &
His Mysterious Voyage

—◦ A.T.

■ In a place called British Columbia, it is hardly surprising that efforts would be made to prove that an Englishman got here first — before other Europeans. Publication of Samuel Bawlf's *The Secret Voyage of Sir Francis Drake 1577–1580* (Douglas & McIntyre) prompted the following essay.

SOON AFTER CHRISTOPHER COLUMBUS became the first accidental European tourist of the Americas, Spain and Portugal were granted exclusive rights to New World territories by the Pope. In defiance of Rome, the Genoese sailor John Cabot promptly reached Newfoundland for England in 1497.

His son Sebastian Cabot went searching for the Northwest Passage for England in 1508. The tiny island realm of England was hoping to compete in the spice race in a Catholics Only sea. The Portuguese were superior mariners but the Spanish led the way, having recently vanquished their Moors and Jews, and terrorized their populace with the Inquisition.

Vasco Núñez de Balboa crossed Panama and found a new ocean in 1513. Nine years later, 18 emaciated members of Ferdinand Magellan's 250-man crew completed the first circumnavigation of the globe. Their captain had been killed by South Sea Islanders. That year the Merchant Adventurers for the Discovery of Regions, Dominions, Islands, and Places Unknown was created with Sebastian Cabot as its governor for life.

By the time Sebastian Cabot died in 1557, the known world had quadrupled in his lifetime. Queen Elizabeth came to power in 1558. Her most influential adviser on navigational matters was a Welsh mathematician and "cosmographer" named Dr. John Dee, who also taught the Queen's most enduring paramour, Robert Dudley. As the Queen's astrologer and astronomer, Dee conveyed the contents of the first map of the known world that was published by his continental associate Abraham Ortelius, a Flemish geographer.

The Ortelius map incorporated the innovative extrapolations of Gerard Mercator as well as the new 1561 theory of Italian cartographer Giacomo Gastaldi who boldly theorized — correctly, as it turned out — that America was separated from Asia at the northern extremity of the Pacific Ocean.

England yearned to discover a Northwest Passage across the top of Canada, and then connect with a hoped-for watery artery between Asia and America. This unseen waterway was called the Strait of Anian (later the Bering Strait, named after the Russian explorer Vitus Bering). If England could control the Strait of Anian, it would control the fastest route to the Orient.

This is where Francis Drake enters the picture. The eldest of twelve brothers, Francis Drake, the Columbus of England, was born in Tavistock, Devon, around 1542. The Drake family had lost property when King Henry VIII founded the Church of England in defiance of Rome. Drake was sent to live with his seafaring kin, the Hawkins family. Leaving Plymouth in 1562, Drake likely accompanied John Hawkins down the Guinea coast to acquire slaves from present-day Sierra Leone.

As a Caribbean slave trader in 1568, Drake was part of Hawkins' flotilla when it was attacked by a superior Spanish force. This clash with

Spain gained Drake the lifelong right to function as a privateer, in essence, a legalized pirate. Drake quickly became famous for his looting of Spanish galleons. He made profitable voyages in 1570 and 1571, trading slaves in the West Indies, then commanded two ships in 1572 to specifically attack the Spanish. Spanish mothers took to frightening their children into good behaviour with tales of "El Draque," the Dragon.

Drake was known as a harsh taskmaster. When one of his brothers died at sea, he proceeded to have the body dissected to find the cause of his death. Impressed by his daring, Queen Elizabeth sent him on a secret mission to plunder Spanish settlements on the Pacific Coast of the New World in 1577.

Of the five ships sent, two had already been abandoned before reaching the southern tip of the South American continent. The remaining three ships passed through the Strait of Magellan. This was new territory for England. Violent storms destroyed one ship; another sailed back to England; Drake was blown far south but travelled back up the coast, preying on the Spanish, stealing maps and ships.

Drake headed north, some claim as far as today's US/Canada border, naming this uncharted realm to the north, New Albion. This land above the 49th parallel was to be eventually called British Columbia. British Drakia might have been more to the point.

Unable to find a passage home via the imagined Strait of Anian, Drake headed westward across the Pacific, through the islands of Indonesia and finally around the Cape of Good Hope at the bottom of Africa. Drake made it back to England by September of 1580, bearing an enormous cache of spices and Spanish booty. Queen Elizabeth knighted Drake aboard the *Golden Hinde* for becoming the first Englishman to fully circumnavigate the world.

The once lowly seaman became mayor of Plymouth in 1581. He became a Member of Parliament in 1584. In 1585 he led a large fleet to the Caribbean to terrorize the ports of Spanish America. Sir Francis Drake's plundering was so successful in the Caribbean that he ruined Spanish credit, decimating the Bank of Spain and nearly breaking the Bank of Venice to which Spain was heavily indebted.

Drake gained permanent heroic status in the annals of English history by playing a major role in the defeat of the once all-powerful Spanish Armada in 1588. But the Spanish navy wasn't completely destroyed. Four Spanish ships made a daring raid on Penzance in Cornwall, destroying the village of Mousehole, in July of 1595.

Drake continued stalking the Spanish. He suggested a raid on Panama, and the Queen agreed. During his fruitless mission, he contracted dysentery ("the bloody flux") at Panama and died on January 29, 1596. Just as Columbus went to his death believing he'd reached Asia, Drake always maintained he'd found the Strait of Anian.

Officially, Francis Drake "dyed without Issue" and was buried at sea.

Samuel Bawlf's *The Secret Voyage of Sir Francis Drake, 1577–1580* is a fascinating, problematic and contentious journey of research and conjecture. It recounts how and why Drake's mid-career quest for the Strait of Anian took him up the Pacific coast to the 48th parallel, and possibly beyond, after which he became the first sea captain to circumnavigate the world.

"Whether Drake reached the coast as far north as the Strait of Juan de Fuca is likely to remain a puzzle," wrote Derek Hayes, author of *Historical Atlas of British Columbia and the Pacific Northwest*, also published by Douglas & McIntyre.

Despite the packaging of his title as a revelation, Bawlf is not the first historian to propose the Drake-came-first idea. Just as the British chauvinists in the former colony of British Honduras have tried gamely for more than a century to convince the world, and themselves, that the present name for the country of Belize is derivative of the surname Wallace, a Scottish pirate — when it's clear the Mayan word *beliz* means "muddy." — Anglophiles in a place that is still called British Columbia have long been apt to claim Drake as their "founder."

Although it's not mentioned anywhere in Bawlf's text, the prolific social reformer A.M. Stephen of Vancouver published his first novel, *The Kingdom of the Sun*, in 1927. It's about a gentleman adventurer named Richard Anson who sailed aboard Drake's *Golden Hinde*, only to be cast away among the Haida and fall in love with a blonde Haida.

"It is a near certainty," writes Derek Hayes, "that the Japanese or Chinese people arrived on the northwest coast long before any European."

Hayes also notes that Spanish galleons laden with spices, silver and bees-wax were making annual voyages to New Spain (Mexico) from the Phil-ippines ever since the Spanish sea captain Alonso de Arellano discovered the Westerlies of the Pacific Ocean in 1564. The Spaniards used the north Pacific to reach Mexico. Ruy Lopez de Villalobos had named the Philip-pines after King Charles' son Philip in 1542, having sailed there from Mexico. In other words, there's a pretty good chance Spaniards grazed the Pacific Coast before Drake.

Drake gave British Columbia its first European-based name — Nova Albion, essentially New England (the white cliffs of Dover, etc.) — but historians agree to disagree about whether or not Drake sailed above the 49th parallel prior to the Greek navigator Juan de Fuca (whose real name was Apostolos Valerianos) in 1592 or 1594, an equally contentious claim.

Naval charts were precious and kept secret during the Elizabethan era. This was especially so with Drake's round-the-world trip. If he discovered the Strait of Anian, his charts and rough maps could not be publicized for fear of Spanish competition and reprisals.

Bawlf's research credibly outlines why an exact accounting of Drake's voyage up the "backside of Canada" was never published in his lifetime. Conflicting depictions of Drake's foray are impressively outlined but the cumulative result will be a tad dizzying to anyone without previous knowledge of the subject.

Bawlf writes, "Immediately upon Drake's return in 1580, Queen Eliza-beth had ordered a ban on publication of any details of his voyage. In time, Drake began giving hand-drawn maps depicting his route around the world to important friends. In an early rendition, drawn with pen and ink on the world map of Abraham Ortelius, his route extended north-ward along the coast of North America to latitude 57 degrees — the latitude of Southern Alaska — before returning south and homeward via the East Indies. Then, with the help of a young Flemish artist named Jodocus Hondius, Drake produced several more maps. On these maps his track northward terminated at a lower latitude, where an inscription read 'turned back on account of the ice,' and then returned southward to a place called Nova Albion."

A lone footnote provides a clue as to why Bawlf's work has such an awkward structure. At one point the story leaps from the southern coast of Mexico in April to the Philippines in November. Complex evidence to support the claim that Bawlf's work is a revelation is mostly placed at the end. "This book draws from my academic work *Sir Francis Drake's Secret Voyage to the Northwest Coast of America in AD 1579. . . .* Since its publication in 2001, I have modified my conclusions in some areas. Therefore, unless otherwise noted this book takes precedence over my earlier work." The reader needs to be a detective to ascertain that *The Secret Voyage* is an effort to popularize the preceding work.

The publisher's audacious claim that Drake definitely reached Alaska (and was therefore the first European to "discover" Canada's western shores) is a commercial pitch as much as it is a verifiable claim. Meanwhile, Drake scholars around the world will be obliged to buy *The Secret Voyage* to evaluate Bawlf's entirely admirable effort to formulate an original but partially speculative perspective.

Bawlf's writing is most enjoyable when he provides details of the heroic 1577–1580 global voyage that took Drake and his Cambridge-educated cleric Francis Fletcher — who kept the journal — to "the very end of the world from us."

Drake departed on December 13, 1577, and quickly reached Morocco, losing a boy overboard en route from the supply ship *Swan*, the first of his many casualties. Drake got lucky in early February when he commandeered a Portuguese ship off the Cape Verde Islands, kidnapping its veteran captain Nuño da Silva who had sailed to Brazil many times since his boyhood. In the process, Drake acquired charts for his Atlantic voyage and soundings for the South American coast as far south as Rio de la Plata. He would employ a similar tactic, with equal success, when he reached the Pacific.

Drake crossed the equator on February 17, 1578. In South America his crew met Indians who never cut their hair, knitting it with ostrich feathers to form a quiver for their arrows. Accusing the troublesome investor Thomas Doughty of treachery, Drake had his adversary executed by axe on July 2, 1578. For food during the voyage, the crew slaughtered sea lions and penguins. They also found the bones of a Spanish mutineer named Gaspar Quesada killed by Magellan in 1522.

With his crew afflicted by scurvy and cold temperatures, Drake discovered that a stew of mussels and seaweed could be restorative. Upon entering the perilous Strait of Magellan, Drake changed the name of his heavily armed flagship from the *Pelican* to the *Golden Hinde*. The land south of the strait was called Tierra del Fuego (land of fires) because Indians had lit fires as Magellan had sailed past. On one day in August, Drake's remaining men slaughtered 3,000 penguins, enough food to last forty days.

After only sixteen days battling the currents and the foul weather, they reached the Pacific on September 6, 1578. For the next fifty days or so, they were beset by storms. They finally set sail for the Kingdom of Peru with eighty men and boys, sailing 1,200 miles without stopping.

On the island of Mocha, at thirty-eight degrees south, initially friendly Indians attacked their landing party, killing several men with a flurry of arrows. "Drake was hit twice, one penetrating his face under his right eye and another creasing his scalp." Fletcher recorded in his journal that no one escaped being hit. One crewman was punctured by twenty-one arrows.

The Spanish were aghast that Drake had become the first English sea captain to replicate Magellan's path. The buildup of Spanish ports and mining from California to Chile had been accomplished primarily via overland routes through Panama.

During his piratical triumphs, Drake took aboard a black slave as his concubine. Maria, as she was named, was "gotten with child between the captain and his men pirates" and she was to be marooned on an Indonesian island to have the child, along with two black slaves for company.

Bawlf's narrative stops at Mexico. Thereafter it becomes a maze of hypothesis and conjecture. Captains Galiano, Quadra and Vancouver become prominent characters, as well as England's main proponent of overseas exploration, Richard Hakluyt. Like a lawyer arguing his case, Bawlf piles up his nautical suppositions with carefully worded sentences. "The evidence in Drake's maps is compelling. . . . Taking soundings, they would have found the channel deep enough for the *Golden Hinde*. . . ."

Anybody can cobble together a serviceable biography of Drake; Bawlf aims higher. He wants to convince his fellow historians to accept the clearly stated claims about Drake made by the publisher without overtly making those claims in the text himself. If the reader starts to feel like his arm is being twisted, it's partly because Bawlf is at such pains to persuade us that Drake was wholly an admirable fellow in the process. If he can misrepresent Drake as a gentleman. . . .

Bawlf is never reticent to quote complimentary assessments of Drake's character. One day Queen Elizabeth met with him an unprecedented nine times, etc. ". . . he seems destined by the Good Lord to achieve great things; perceptive and intelligent by nature, his practical abilities astonishing, his memory acute, his skill in managing a fleet virtually unique. . . ."

No doubt there exists an entirely laudatory text about Neil Armstrong, too, as there are entirely laudatory books about Columbus and Cortés. Anyone reading *The Secret Voyage* who is new to the subject of Drake would have an extremely difficult time learning and remembering Drake began his career as a slave trader. "Drake was a remarkably gentle corsair," Bawlf writes, "in comparison to the French pirates." He goes on to say, "Drake had gained favourable reputation among the Spaniards," and adds, "for the civility and kindness he exhibited toward his captives."

In fact, the romantic ethic of "one for all and all for one" was not for Francis Drake. He was a charming, dastardly man, loathed by many in London and around the world.

One famous incident in which Drake's character was called into question is skirted by Bawlf. As a young man, Drake was at the helm of *Judith*, two days after entering the principal Mexican port of San Juan de Ulúa in 1568. Hawkins' out-manned flotilla was attacked by the Spanish with terrifying results. Drake fled the harbour, leaving hundreds of desperate English sailors stranded. "The *Judith* forsooke us in our great myserie," said one of Hawkins' men. But that's not a quote that appears in Bawlf's version of events. When reading Bawlf's account, it isn't possible to deduce that Drake was vilified long afterwards for betraying his companions.

"Only the *Minion*, and Francis Drake's *Judith* were sufficiently intact to be sailed," he records. ". . . Hawkins and the crew of the *Jesus* hastily transferred to the *Minion* and then Drake led the way out of the harbor. Sometime in the night, however, the two ships became separated."

Emerging Protestant attitudes stressed individual achievement — if you could make money, this meant God favoured you. Drake won God's favour as a deadly privateer. He was the harbinger of a new age, essentially a self-made man. As a pitchman for Drake, Bawlf can be criticized, but his research and long-term regard for his subject have generated a must-have volume for any serious BC history buff.

[2003]

Seven Reasons Why Drake Didn't Reach British Columbia in 1579

—◌ EDWARD VON DER PORTEN

■ Edward Von der Porten, a museum director and the president of the Drake
  Navigators Guild, is one of many naval scholars who have taken extreme
  objection to Samuel Bawlf's *The Secret Voyage of Sir Francis Drake* (2003),
  and its marketing, which leads one to assume Francis Drake was the first
  European to reach British Columbia. "Bawlf's book is fantasy on the same
  plane as Gavin Menzies' *1421*, Vikings in Minnesota and ancient astronauts,"
  says Von der Porten. "Serious research has long resolved the issues of where
  Drake travelled in the Pacific, and British Columbia could not have been a
  place he visited." Here is Von der Porten's rebuttal of the Bawlf thesis.

1. Bawlf brings Drake to the Northwest Coast from Guatulco, Mexico, by
using distances in leagues given in the accounts of the voyage. The mea-
surement of the league used by Bawlf is the modern league of 18,228 feet,
which would place Drake on the coast in southern Washington, not Vancouver Island. However, Drake used the Elizabethan league of 15,000
feet, which would put him on the coast in southern Oregon, the latitude

accepted by a broad consensus of modern scholars. *Drake never reached the coast of British Columbia.*

2. Bawlf states that Drake sailed 2,000 miles in forty-four days along the shores of southern Alaska, British Columbia, Washington and Oregon, and made discoveries that later explorers took twenty years to work out. He allows ten days for stops, leaving thirty-four days of sailing time. Travelling day and night, his average speed would have had to be 2.45 knots, or 58.8 miles per day. The *Golden Hinde* averaged three to four knots in the open ocean in good conditions with favourable winds. Along the shore, Drake could have operated only in daylight. Allowing for contrary winds and currents, unpredictable tide races, unknown shoals and pinnacle rocks, fog, rain, and all the other vicissitudes of sailing along complex and dangerous unknown coasts and in narrow waterways among islands and peninsulas in one of the coldest years of the Little Ice Age, his average speed could not have reached one knot in daylight — well under 20 miles per day. *Bawlf's idea that Drake explored 2,000 miles of the northwest coast in thirty-four days is impossible.*

3. Bawlf gives Drake forty-four days to explore the coast by accepting the date Drake arrived on the coast, which is given in the surviving Elizabethan accounts of the expedition. This is June 3, 1579. Bawlf, however, changes the date when Drake ended his exploration and arrived at his Port of *Nova Albion* from June 17 to July 17. Then he changes Drake's departure date from the port from July 23 to August 23. However, Drake visited a group of islands just after leaving his port, according to the accounts, and named them the Isles of Saint James. Saint James' Day is July 25. So Drake did not leave the islands on August 25 as Bawlf claims, but on July 25. The calendar as given in the contemporary accounts is the correct one. This leaves Drake fourteen days — not forty-four — to carry out his explorations between his arrival on the coast and his arrival at the port. With no stops, his day-and-night speed to travel 2,000 miles would have had to be 5.95 knots average, or 142.8 miles per day in a three-to-four-knot ship capable of less than one knot in daylight along an unknown shore. *For Drake to explore 2,000 miles of the northwest coast in fourteen days — the amount of time he had available to spend on exploration — is impossible.*

4. The Native-American peoples Drake met were described in great detail in the accounts. Bawlf claims Drake met the peoples who inhabited the shore from southern Alaska to central Oregon: northwest-coast peoples with huge cedar canoes, split-plank communal houses and totems. No such peoples or artifacts are mentioned in the accounts. Ethnographers have shown that the people Drake met at his port were the Coast Miwok People, a California group living at and near latitude 38 degrees north who had a completely different lifestyle than the northwest coast peoples. Drake's chroniclers could not have described the costumes, ceremonies, artifacts, words and lifeways of a people they had not seen. *Bawlf cannot move a Native-American people north 400 nautical miles.*

5. Drake's port of *Nova Albion* is given by Bawlf as Whale Cove, Oregon. This site does not have the Native Americans, the prominent white cliffs, the offshore Islands of Saint James, the beach-level fortification location, explorer-period artifacts, an open-bay anchorage adjacent to the sheltered careening port, the characteristics shown in Drake's drawing of the port, a safe location to careen the *Golden Hinde*, or reasonable safety of entrance or exit. Whale Cove is not even mentioned in the modern *Coast Pilot*. *Whale Cove could not have been Drake's port.*

6. Bawlf ignores most of the evidence in the accounts and early maps, and claims those few pieces of evidence he deems "true" have been changed following a series of "rules" created by an Elizabethan conspiracy which he has decoded. Yet the accounts of Drake's voyage have long been shown to be remarkably straightforward, detailed and accurate — notably by English scholar Michael Turner, who has located and confirmed by personal field work more than ninety-five locations visited by Drake. *Bawlf provides no evidence to support his claim of a vast Elizabethan conspiracy.*

7. Bawlf apparently is not aware of much of the modern research about Drake in the North Pacific, as his bibliography does not mention numerous publications known to most scholars of the field. These publications analyze much evidence that Bawlf does not even mention in his book. *Bawlf does not deal with a large body of evidence and analysis about Drake's voyage to the west coast of North America.*

[2004]

Frances Barkley:
First Female Invader

—ᵒ A.T.

■ Frances Barkley can be regarded as the first female author of British Columbia, although it took two centuries for her words to be widely circulated. She recorded her views of British Columbia in 1787. Her memoirs entitled *Reminiscences* were published as part of *The Remarkable World of Frances Barkley 1769–1845* (Gray's 1978), edited by Beth Hill. An expanded version of *The Remarkable World of Frances Barkley* (Heritage) has been prepared by Cathy Converse.

FRANCES BARKLEY WAS BORN in Bridgewater, Somersetshire, England, in 1769, as Frances Hornby Trevor, daughter of an English chaplain who moved his family to Europe in 1775 where he became rector of a new Protestant Church at Ostend in 1783. Educated at a French Catholic convent, she was a student of French who also learned sewing, embroidery and cooking. One of her sisters married Captain James Cook. At age seventeen, she married twenty-six-year-old Charles William Barkley, an East Indian Company sea captain, on October 17, 1786, at Ostend.

The young Captain Barkley opted to sail under the Austrian colours of the Austrian East Indian Company in an attempt to circumvent the high fees demanded by the two English monopolies. These were the East India Company, Charles Barkley's former employer, and the South Sea Company. The former controlled trade in Asia; the latter controlled the Pacific trade on the West Coast of North America from Cape Horn to the Arctic.

The name of Barkley's ship, the *Loudon*, was changed to the *Imperial Eagle* prior to the couple's embarkation on November 24, 1786, just five weeks after the marriage ceremony. Theirs would be an unprecedented honeymoon cruise. Despite a bout of rheumatic fever for Captain Barkley, their voyage went well, and they soon reached the Americas at Brazil.

The *Imperial Eagle* then arrived at Nootka Sound on the west coast of Vancouver Island in June of 1787. Nootka Sound was also called King George's Sound by the English. Nootka is an English term. In 1778, when Captain Cook initially dropped anchor in Resolution Cove off Bligh Island, the local Mowachaht Indians had approached in canoes calling out, "Itchme nutka! Itchme nutka!" They were saying "go around, go around." Cook had misunderstood their inducements to sail his two ships around Bligh Island to a better anchorage at their village at Yuquot. He had assumed they were trying to introduce themselves — as the Nootka.

At 400 tons, the *Imperial Eagle* was the largest ship to enter Friendly Cove (or Yuquot) but it's more likely the Nootka Indians, or Nuu-Chah-Nulth, were more impressed by Frances Barkley's extraordinary red-gold hair. Legend has it within the Barkley family that her tresses saved the day when the Barkleys were later captured by hostile South Sea natives. Curious women among their captors supposedly loosed her hair "which fell like a shower of gold," whereupon the astonished onlookers presumed she must be divine. Frances then ordered their release. No mention is made of such dramatics in Frances Barkley's *Reminiscences*, penned when she was age 66, so such stories are likely apocryphal, but possibly indicative of the sensation her appearance must have caused.

During their month-long stay at Nootka, Frances Barkley was much impressed by chief Maquinna and his management of the fur trade. The

Imperial Eagle acquired 700 prime skins, and many more of inferior quality, all worth a great fortune for sale in the Orient. They did so with the assistance of John Mackay, an Irishman who had been left behind at Nootka the summer before due to illness ("purple fever"). Mackay is a little-known figure in BC history, who has the distinction of being the first year-round European resident. Mackay had initially gained favour with Maquinna, having helped to cure one of his daughters of an illness, but he was later beaten and banished for having stepped over Maquinna's sleeping child, breaking a local taboo. A shattered man who barely survived the winter, Mackay would last be seen in Bombay, where he languished as an incoherent drunk.

The Barkleys sailed south and named Barkley Sound, Hornby Peak, Frances Island, Trevor Channel, Loudoun Channel, Cape Beale and Imperial Eagle Channel. In honour of the local chief, Captain Barkley also named Wickaninnish Sound, now called Clayoquot Sound. Six of their party were killed by Indians at the mouth of the Strait of Juan de Fuca on July 24, 1787. Depressed by this encounter, the Barkleys set sail for China and reached Macao in December.

During formal trading procedures in Macao — which proved successful — the Barkleys bought an ornate bamboo chair that has survived their journeys. This chair is now the property of the Centennial Museum in Vancouver.

Having made a profit of £10,000 for his backers, Captain Barkley proceeded to the island of Mauritius, off Madagascar, where he first learned the East India Company was initiating legal action against the owners of the *Imperial Eagle*. The owners, including fur trader John Meares, decided to sell the *Imperial Eagle* to avoid legal consequences, thereby breaking their contract with Captain Barkley. The Barkleys stayed for more than a year in the French enclave of Mauritius where Frances Barkley gave birth to their first child, a son. Captain Barkley sailed to India where the *Imperial Eagle* was confiscated. He sued for damages, having invested much of his own money in properly outfitting the ship. Captain Barkley received an arbitration settlement for the loss of his ten-year contract but this was insufficient consolation.

The devious Meares gained possession of Barkley's nautical gear as well as his valuable seafaring journal. The likes of Robert Haswell and George Dixon condemned Meares for failing to credit the use of Captain Barkley's charts in his publications. Maquinna called Meares "Aita-aita Meares," which means "the lying Meares."

Defrauded by Meares, having lost the *Imperial Eagle*, and burdened with a newborn, the Barkleys tried to return to England but were shipwrecked near Holland on an American ship. The Americans abandoned them on the sinking vessel. They finally reached Portsmouth two years after their embarkation from Ostend.

Undeterred, the Barkleys conceived a second voyage to Alaska seven months later, to be made via India. During their eleven-month voyage to Calcutta, Barkley gave birth to a baby girl during a violent gale as they were rounding the Cape of Good Hope in 1791. "Nothing would be easy in this environment; even washing diapers presented a challenge," Beth Hill wrote. "Fresh water was always at a premium so washing in saltwater would be the norm. Salt-encrusted diapers would have caused boils and open sores which do not heal easily, and infection often followed. Frances writes none of this in her *Reminiscences*."

The Barkleys left Calcutta on December 29, 1791, having purchased the 80-ton brig *Halcyon*. Frances Barkley had the option of remaining in Bengal "where I was to have Servants, Palanqueens and every Luxery," but she resolutely insisted on accompanying her husband, "much to the satisfaction of My Husband, who never thought of being separated from me." Others called it madness.

The infant at Frances Barkley's breast would die "and became the Victim of our folly" during this second voyage. "A Leaden Box was prepared for her remains in order that they be kept until we could inter her in consecrated ground in some Dutch settlement," Frances Barkley wrote.

Attempts to trade in Siberia on this second voyage were stymied by Russian officialdom. Similar resistance occurred in the realm of the fearsome Tlingit First Nation where Frances Barkley, in 1792, became the first European woman to visit Alaska. Then, after wintering at "Owyhee" (Hawaii) with fewer pelts than hoped, the *Halycon* left for China in March of 1793. Only when they reached Mauritius did they learn that France and England were once again at war.

The French confiscated the *Halcyon*, and the English temporarily became prisoners. An American sailed the *Halcyon* to the US. The Barkleys eventually found a ride to the US but by then their ship was lost. They reached England in November of 1794 on the *Amphion*. Captain Barkley learned of the presence of the *Halcyon* in Boston and returned there to regain ownership years later.

The Barkleys raised a family in England where Captain Barkley died on May 16, 1832. Four years later, Frances Barkley began writing her fragmented memoirs in 1836, partially to counteract the false claims of Meares. Her *Reminiscences* — mostly written from memory — is housed at the Provincial Archives. The whereabouts of her original sea diary remains a mystery.

Frances Barkley died in 1845. She spent six and a half years at sea, losing one child in the process, but there isn't a single complaint or objection in her memoir about the conditions and disappointments she endured. The Barkleys' attachment to one another seemingly grew in response to the adversities they faced.

[2003]

Who's Who of the Last Coast

—∽ A.T.

■ A long-serving president of the Spanish Pacific Historical Society, former museum and archives director Robin Inglis has untangled the fascinating blend of characters and events that were major influences on the early history of the last temperate coastline to be placed on the world map. It's easy to predict that Inglis' *Historical Dictionary of the Discovery and Exploration of the Northwest Coast of America* will gradually become a required reference work, stored on the same shelf as the *Encyclopedia of BC*, Chuck Davis' Vancouver history volumes or Jean Barman's *The West Beyond the West*.

WHEN YOU GO TO A hockey or baseball game, there's generally a program that provides the names and numbers of the players to enhance the meaning of the contest, to make the encounter into a better story. Similarly, if you go to the theatre, or open a Russian novel, there's generally a list of characters provided at the outset to prevent you from losing your way.

Robin Inglis' mouthful-titled *Historical Dictionary of the Discovery and*

Exploration of the Northwest Coast of America now provides a similar orientation service to untangle the fascinating blend of male and female characters and events that were formative influences on the early history of the last temperate coastline to be placed on the world map. For a succinct endorsement of this volume, one cannot do much better than cheer, "It's about time!"

After four years of concision, Inglis' *Northwest Coast*, at 428 pages, could have been twice as long, but it would have been half as valuable. Condensed-but-all-inclusive, this authoritative guide casts a gigantic biographical net over a dizzying range of little-known Russian, British, French, Spanish and American mariners and traders.

The first European known to have visited British Columbia waters was Juan Pérez, sailing from the San Blas naval base, south of San Diego, in 1774, to Langara Island (Haida Gwaii) and then south to the mouth of Nootka Sound (eastern Vancouver Island). He was followed by Captain Bodega y Quadra in 1775, and more famously by Captain James Cook in

A cautionary tale.

1778 (including young officers George Vancouver and William Bligh of *Mutiny on the Bounty* fame).

Beyond that, most British Columbians know next-to-nothing, or simply nothing, about the first invaders of coastal First Nations lands, so Inglis has provided more than 400 cross-referenced entries, along with a cogent introduction, maps and illustrations, an extensive bibliography (with advice on essential reference works) and an engaging chronology of events dating from the Treaty of Tordesillas in 1494 (when the Pope divided the undiscovered world between Spain and Portugal) and the purchase of Russian America by the United States in 1867.

Whew. Inglis' streamlined omnibus is the fourth volume in a series of historical dictionaries of discovery and exploration edited by Jon Woronoff, who has noted there has been a tendency towards scholarly patriotism — or just laziness — in works about the North Pacific Coast. "Thus the greatest merit of the author," according to Woronoff, "is to have placed equal and fair emphasis on all of the actors, including the Spanish, French and Russian, who all too often and unfairly come in a very distant second to the British and Americans."

This is true. The dozens of Russian names we encounter are made pleasing to learn when we know their numbers, the positions they play, their stats. Inglis has expanded North Pacific history into a new league. Who knew that Kirill Khlebnikov (1785–1838) was the official historian of the Russian-American Company? And that in 1953 his private papers revealed the long-lost journal of Vasilii Khromchenko, navigator for the Otto von Kotzebue expedition, 1815–1818?

Better yet, this compendium is as trustworthy as it is culturally unbiased. As the guiding force behind Vancouver-based *Instituto de Historia del Pacifico Español* (Spanish Pacific History Society), Inglis, former director of the Vancouver Maritime Museum and North Vancouver Museum and Archives, has been able to benefit from the intelligence and knowledge of an impressive list of contacts such as Donald Cutter, Barry Gough, Glyndwr Williams, Derek Hayes, John Kendrick and Freeman Tovell — to mention only a few.

Perhaps as a consequence of his intimidating peer group, Inglis assiduously avoids going out on limbs of scholarly conjecture. As to whether or not the mysterious Greek-born Apostolos Valerianos, better known as

Juan de Fuca, might have reached a broad inlet between latitudes of 47 and 48 degrees in 1592, Inglis will only condescend to agree this intriguing scenario "is not entirely outside the realm of possibility."

Inglis' restraint in not including titillating tidbits is admirable. For instance, he limits his entry on the fantastical life of John Ledyard, "The American Marco Polo," to four paragraphs, and he does not accord much historical status to the bizarre misadventures of John Mackay, the first European to live year-round at Friendly Cove and Tahsis with Chief Maquinna, from 1786–1787. The famous captivity of John Jewitt from 1803–1805 is worthy of just one paragraph.

Clearly Inglis is serving the interests of posterity, not *People* magazine. But he does play a few favourites. Notably he trumpets the work of German botanist Georg Wilhelm Steller, who documented the sea cow or northern manatee, *Hydrodamalis gigas*, before it was hunted to extinction by Russians in the late 18th century. (British Columbia's provincial bird was later named *Cyanocittus stelleri* or Steller's Jay, another tidbit excluded by Inglis, who is clearly writing for an international readership.)

Entries range far beyond maritime explorers such as the ineffectual Vitus Bering and the under-appreciated George Vancouver to include overland explorers (David Thompson, Simon Fraser, etc.), sea otters, scientists, Nootka Crisis, Shumagin Islands, San Juan Border Dispute, Chief Maquinna (there were likely two Maquinnas between Cook's arrival in 1778 and Jewitt's captivity) and the far-sighted Thomas Jefferson (who sponsored the Lewis & Clark expedition, after being encouraged by Ledyard).

The art of concision is seldom rewarded, or even mentioned — but *Northwest Coast of America* is an artful undertaking. (You have to know a lot before you can figure out what parts to leave out.) One example of Inglis' succinctness, within the book's 400-plus entries, is a rare mention of a female personality, Frances Barkley. The only two women with separate entries are Catherine the Great and Natalia Shelikhov, wife of the Russian explorer Grigory Shelikhov.

Charles William Barkley (1759–1832) sailed in the service of the East India Company (EIC) before resigning in 1786 to make a trading voyage (sponsored surreptitiously by a number of Company directors) to the Northwest Coast in the English-built *Imperial Eagle*.

The ship left Ostend in November, flying the Austrian flag to avoid the monopoly regulations of the EIC in the North Pacific. At 400 tons with twenty guns, she was the largest vessel to visit the coast up to that time.

A month earlier Barkley had married a young wife, Frances, the first European woman known to visit British Columbia, and whose *Reminiscences* (first published in 1978) provide an intriguing insight into life and activities aboard an 18th-century trading vessel.

The *Imperial Eagle* reached Nootka Sound in June 1787. Here Barkley met John Mackay, a ship's surgeon who had been left there the previous summer by another trader, James Strange. Mackay offered valuable information about local trading activities and the geography of the coast, which suggested that Nootka was on an island, not the American continent. As a result, Barkley sailed his ship south and traded successfully in Clayoquot Sound and another large indentation in the coast, which he named Barkley Sound after himself.

Proceeding farther south he was astonished to find, at the end of July, that he was off the entrance to a great strait, which he promptly named after the legendary navigator Juan de Fuca, who was said to have discovered a strait in the same latitude on the American west coast in 1592. He was particularly surprised because the strait's existence had been discounted by James Cook a mere nine years earlier in 1778.

Tragedy then befell the voyage when, near Destruction Island and the mouth of the Hoh River in Washington, six men landed a small boat but were promptly killed by local natives.

Barkley sailed immediately for Canton to sell his cargo of furs. There he found not only an already saturated market but also, more ominously, that the EIC had discovered the threat to its monopoly. As he planned a second voyage, his partners disassociated themselves from the venture to save their positions; their agents sold the *Imperial Eagle* and Barkley's charts, journals and stores were acquired by John Meares. Meares used the information in the account of his own voyages to the Northwest Coast, published in 1790, although he did credit Barkley with the discovery of the Strait of Juan de Fuca.

[2009]

The Enigma of Cannibalism

—◦ A.T.

I went all around the world to find food.
I went all around the world to find human flesh.
I went all around the world to find human heads.
I went all around the world to find corpses.

— *Hamatsa Song, recorded by Franz Boas 1895*

THE FIRST EUROPEAN to declare in print that Northwest Coast Aboriginals engaged in cannibalism was the German sailor Heinrich Zimmerman who served under Captain James Cook aboard the *Resolution*.
In 1781 Zimmerman published his journal in which he stated that the
Mowachaht at Nootka Sound had "dried human flesh which they ate
with relish and which they wished us to try."

One of the first English-speaking mariners to make much the same
claim was an American sailor on the same voyage, John Ledyard. In his
1783 journal, Ledyard recalled that hospitable Aboriginals had offered a
roasted human arm and that he had tasted it. "We intimated to our hosts
that what we had tasted was bad," he wrote.

When Captain Cook's journal was published posthumously in 1784, describing his month-long stay at Nootka Sound in 1778, he described considerable trade in body parts but stopped short of ascribing the practice of cannibalism because he himself hadn't witnessed it.

James Strange, the second English captain to visit Nootka, recorded meeting Chief Maquinna's son in law, Callicum, who tried to sell him three hands and a head. Callicum supposedly told Strange these items were good for eating. Callicum "very composedly put one of the hands in his mouth and, stripping it through his teeth, tore off a considerable piece of flesh, which he immediately devoured with much apparent relish."

As a twenty-one-year-old ensign under Strange, Alexander Walker later interviewed John Mackay, the first European to see how the Indians at Nootka lived during the winter months when their most important ceremonies were held. Walker's much revised journal, unpublished until 1982, offers rare eyewitness testimonies.

"We saw many bare skulls in the possession of these people and one [with] the flesh and hair upon it; and which was still bloody. They ate part of this raw before us, and as usual expressed the highest relish for the food. Upon another occasion they produced an arm half roasted, feeding on it in the same manner."

In 1788, the English fur trader John Meares recorded his outright suspicions of cannibalism. "We were very much disposed to believe that Maquinna himself was a cannibal." Meares learned from two chiefs that Maquinna feasted on a slave "every moon." A year later in 1789, Spanish explorer Esteban José Martínez reached Nootka, where his crew noted Maquinna ate little boys and girls captured in war.

Then in March of 1803, Maquinna massacred the crew of the English brigantine *Boston* except for two sailors, an older seaman named John Thompson and a 19-year-old armourer, John Jewitt. The journal Jewitt published after his two years in captivity contains the first detailed descriptions of how Maquinna's winter rituals and grisly practices might, in fact, have been religious ceremonies.

In first compiling the history of European perceptions of allegedly cannibalistic behaviour among coastal Indians, Jim McDowell, in *Hamatsa: The Enigma of Cannibalism on the Pacific Northwest Coast* (Ronsdale), repeatedly advises the reader to mistrust the sensational viewpoints of early explorers and cautions the reader to consider motives for apparently bloodthirsty behaviour.

McDowell takes great care to stress that ritual cannibalism is very different from gustatory cannibalism. "When most of us encounter the word cannibalism, we tend to assume that the only practice being addressed is the one implied by the term's literal meaning: human use of human beings as tasteful, nourishing food.

"But this is just one of the forms man-eating appears to have assumed in the distant past. Known as *gustatory* or *dietary cannibalism*, it seems to have occurred rarely, if at all, in certain isolated, widely separated, mainly prehistoric cultures. . . .

"We still tend to equate cannibalism only with isolated, culturally restricted acts of eating human flesh. But, in its ritualistic forms, such behaviour — both simulated and actual — conveyed profound metaphors for timeless metaphysical messages about spiritual renewal."

After analyzing early explorers' accounts with skepticism, McDowell notes the first person to conduct an ethnographic study of Northwest Coast Indians was Gilbert Malcolm Sproat in 1861. After living with Indians in the Alberni area and learning their language, Sproat was similarly convinced, from hearsay and from observing ritualistic sacrifices, that cannibalism existed.

Much-travelled Methodist minister and mariner Thomas Crosby first reported in his memoirs the tradition of the hamatsa: ceremonial man-eaters in secret societies. Geologist and ethnographer George Dawson found remnants of cannibalistic rites, and Norwegian ethnographer Johan Adrian Jacobsen also observed cannibal dance ceremonies in Quatsino Sound.

McDowell uses the first half of his book to very cautiously lead the reader to presume hamatsa ceremonies existed as a sophisticated form of ritual cannibalism. He chiefly values the extensive documentation of the coast's most important anthropologist, Franz Boas, who traced aboriginal history, using Native informants, back to the beginning of the 19th century. Between 1886 and 1931 Boas extensively documented Kwakiutl culture and mythology, claiming the custom of devouring men was introduced by the Heilstuq or Heiltsuk that resided from Gardner Canal to Rivers Inlet.

McDowell reveals how some scholars have "sanitized" Boas' field studies, which were often generated by George Hunt, the son of a Tlingit noblewoman and a Scot who worked for the Hudson's Bay Company. After visiting a Kwakiutl village in 1900, Hunt, a special constable, was himself charged with, and acquitted of, violating a clause of the anti-potlatch law that prohibited the "mutilation of human bodies."

Boas and Hunt outlined the hamatsa traditions derived from the legend of Man Eater at the North End of the World. In addition, George Hunt provided extensive personal evidence of contemporary hamatsa ceremonies, including testimony from Hamasaka, the principal hamatsa at Fort Rupert, that he had participated in thirty-two corpse-eating feasts.

In 1902, Hunt photographed a re-enactment of a hamatsa initiate ceremony. Relying on Boas' documentation, controversial ethno photographer Edward S. Curtis also staged a series of photos between 1910 and 1915 to illustrate the legacy of cannibal practices. In 1930, Boas tried to incorporate similar scenes into his documentary film, *The Kwakiutl of British Columbia*.

But perhaps Jim McDowell's chief informant for *Hamatsa: Enigma of Cannibalism* is Sigmund Freud. After providing a worldly overview of the historical taboo of cannibalism — in which anthropologist Peggy Reeves Sanday notes that the attribution of cannibalism is sometimes a projection of moral superiority — McDowell cites Freud's 1913 work, *Totem and Taboo*, in which Freud theorizes that primordial incest is the foundation of totemism and religion.

Freud examined the psychoanalytic origins of cannibalism by suggesting that when the earliest stage of human society was the "primal horde," the violent and jealous father kept all the females for himself and drove his sons into exile and sexual celibacy. Taking their revenge, the rebellious sons killed and ate the primal father.

"The violent primal father had doubtless been the feared and envied model of each of the brothers," said Freud. "In the act of devouring him they accomplished their identification with him, and each of them acquired a portion of his strength."

Freud suggests the sons regularly commemorated and replicated the original patricide by ritual slaughter and consumption of a totemic animal. According to McDowell, Freud said in 1946 that this mythical totemic feast, "which is perhaps mankind's earliest festival," marked the crucial turning point in the evolutionary development of human beings — the "beginning . . . of social organization, or moral restrictions, and of religion."

In further chapters McDowell examines how Freud's viewpoint enhances the significance of ceremonial cannibalism. "Totemic religion," said Freud, "not only comprised expressions of remorse and attempts at atonement, it also served as a remembrance of the triumph over the father. Satisfaction over that triumph led to the institution of the memorial festival of the totem meal, in which the restrictions of deferred obedience no longer held."

If this all seems far out, just think of Catholics eating wafers and drinking Christ's blood in church. Echoing some of the findings of American anthropologist Stanley Walans, McDowell examines how food, as the metaphor of social relationships, is incorporated into hamatsa ceremonies for religious purposes.

McDowell concludes that the winter potlatch, highlighted by the cannibal dance, unites all creatures within a unitary, coherent system of behaviour that reflects a basic morality. "The Kwakiutl," he writes, "believed that humans survive only because the spirits gave them food. In return, people were obligated to give lives, in the form of human souls, to the spirits. The transformation of rebirth occurred through two processes: vomit and fire."

He posits that the cannibal dance ceremony — still practised in derivative forms — re-enacts the primal conflict between hunger and its submission to collective ritual, between narcissistic desire and socialization. "The taming of hamatsas," McDowell says, "resembles the socialization of children."

Walens points out that once humans have reaffirmed their willingness to allow the reborn spirit to live among them, the hamatsa retires to the sacred inner room and vomits up the transformed flesh, "an act symbolic of his transformation from a destructive to a creative being."

For anyone who might wish to restrict or misinterpret McDowell's ambitious book by sensationalizing its contents or intent, three sentences on page 234 are important:

"Kwakiutl cannibalism," McDowell writes, "did not represent the type of gastronomic custom that may have existed among certain aboriginal societies in Africa or the South Sea Islands. On the contrary, the eating of human flesh was abhorrent to all Northwest Coast Indians. It was precisely this loathing that made the gruesome rite all the more powerful."

McDowell compares the hamatsa to medieval knights sent to slay dragons: emissaries sent to confront the embodiments of darkness, the forces we fear most. Because he feels contemporary First World society is well on its way to devouring itself, McDowell believes ritual cannibalism — as a metaphor for our condition — provides a valuable perspective from which we may be able to forge new respect for our environment.

[1997]

The Archaic Name of British Columbia

—◦ A.T.

■ As Shadbolt Fellow at Simon Fraser University in 2007, Alan Twigg organized a conference on BC publishing and writing at the university called Reckoning 07. BC BookWorld simultaneously provided a forum for essays on culture and literature, including this inquiry into the relevance of the name "British Columbia."

THE NAME OF BRITISH COLUMBIA is a literary issue that a mature society ought to be able to at least consider. The very idea of possibly changing the name of British Columbia is cultural heresy in some people's minds, but surely it's about time for some sober reflection on this issue.

As Peter Newman has observed, roast beef is now an ethnic dish. If you're a Chinese British Columbian, or someone from one of our First Nations, or, let's say, someone who has Japanese or German or Dutch or Bengali ancestors, does the name British Columbia sit well with you?

I have five generations of ancestors who have approved of the name

British Columbia — but increasingly I ask myself why other places on the planet have seen fit to jettison that adjective British, rejecting their colonial names and redefining themselves, whereas we haven't even talked about it. The archaic name of British Columbia is not a burning issue. It doesn't haunt anyone's dreams. Of course it would be costly to change it. And we'd have difficulty deciding on a new name. But it's a literary issue that has intrigued me for decades.

Anyone interested in onomastics — the study of names and naming practices — might be entertained by a brief enquiry into the origins of our province's name. But before we consider finding a new name, it's a good idea to understand how we got the old one.

To understand the genesis of the name British Columbia, you can consult Jean Barman's *The West Beyond the West* or perhaps the Akriggs' *British Columbia Chronicle, 1847–1871*. Or you can contact the experts on naming things, the folks who are members of the Canadian Society for the Study of Names or the American Names Society founded in 1951. To begin, an argument can be made that British Columbia is *not* derived from Christopher Columbus.

Yes, Queen Victoria reputedly chose the name British Columbia by joining the adjective British to the northerly portion of the Columbia fur trading district.

Yes, the Columbia fur trading district, in turn, derived its name from the Columbia River.

Yes, the river was named on May 12, 1792, after the ship *Columbia Rediviva*, which sailed under the American sea captain Robert Gray, who was allegedly the first "white" man to navigate up the mouth of that river on May 11, 1792 (a Spaniard got there before him, but that's usually overlooked). But Gray's ship was not necessarily named in honour of Columbus, the explorer, as most people would guess. Why would American puritans in the mid 1700s want to name their ship after a little-known Italian Catholic? It is more likely they chose to honour one of the three patron saints of Ireland, St. Columb, or St. Columba, a great Irish sailor who had the gumption to found a monastery on the island of Iona in Scotland in the sixth century A.D.

Most British Columbians don't know, and they couldn't care less, that a British monarch combined an adjective that connotes imperialism with a noun derived from an Irish saint to define where and who we are.

America, after all, is named for the Italian merchant Amerigo Vespucci simply because a German cartographer named Martin Waldseemüller produced a world map in 1507 that named the newly discovered continent after Vespucci's first name. The name of the Pacific Ocean is similarly ludicrous. After Magellan successfully navigated those straits near the bottom of the Americas, he happened to reach the new ocean on a day when it was unusually calm, or "passive," hence the name Pacific was born — an absurdity if you've ever ventured very far from this coast in any kind of boat.

"I think it is unlikely Queen Victoria (who was thirty-nine in 1858 and given to strong opinions on such issues as naming and protocol) wanted to name the new colony after an American ship or an Irish saint," writes Howard White, publisher of the *Encyclopedia of British Columbia*. "I think she had in mind that "Columbia" was appropriate because it was the name used by geographers for all of the new lands discovered by Columbus (it was commonly used as a rhetorical name for the US).

"Sticking 'British' in front was consistent with the naming method used all over the empire, as in 'British East Africa,' 'British Guiana,' 'British Honduras,' etc. As the Akriggs wrote, 'It preserved the name of the empire lost to the Americans and at the same time it served as a reminder that a portion of it had been saved, to grow and mature in another tradition.'

"I am sure this is closer to the Queen's thinking and that of her advisors than the idea she was naming it after the Columbia River or the Columbia District, which by this time had been formally ceded to the US. So I think it is a bit of a short circuit to say BC was named after an American ship and an Irish saint. There is a connection, but it is not the main one."

Okay, okay. The name of British Columbia is acceptable if we want to respect the wishes of a British queen who never saw the place. And if the majority of British Columbians want to be defined as a British post-colonialists.

[2007]

Top Ten BC Characters

⟶ GEORGE WOODCOCK

■ George Woodcock, *BC BookWorlds*' first poetry columnist, was variously described as "quite possibly the most civilized man in Canada," "by far Canada's most prolific writer," "Canada's Tolstoy," "a regional, national and international treasure" and "a kind of John Stuart Mill of dedication to intellectual excellence and the cause of human liberty." In addition to his literary work, George will be remembered alongside his wife, Ingeborg, for their dedication to charitable work, including the establishment of non-profit organizations such as Trans Himalayan Aid Society and *Canada India Village Aid*, as well as a multi-million dollar endowment fund to benefit Canadian writers in distress, administered by The Writers Trust. The following essay is the last column George Woodcock submitted to *BC BookWorld* before his death on January 28, 1995.

NO MATTER HOW MANY colourful and important individuals have appeared in BC history, I must begin my list of significant characters by saying the ultimate hero west of the Rockies has always been the ever-changing Everyman whom "historic" figures sometimes represent.

Thus if I begin by mentioning the Native chief Maquinna — who was encountered by so many Europeans in the late 18th and early 19th centuries (likely Maquinna was not a single individual but at least two men bearing the same title in succession) — I'm really referring to the complex of Native life that Maquinna represents.

The importance of George Vancouver lies in the fact that he charted so much of the "new" world of the north Pacific (new to white society). But I cannot detach Vancouver from his Spanish rival and friend Bodega (whom we wrongly call Quadra) or from the many minor officers and seamen who rowed their boats into obscure inlets and many of whose names — English and Spanish — define the features of our coast.

James Douglas is another person who stands out in early BC history. He was the man who picked the site of Victoria, transferred the Hudson's Bay Company's headquarters there from American territory, governed the colony of Vancouver Island and virtually founded the colony of British Columbia, presiding over its transition from a fur-trading domain into a mining colony.

Yet behind Douglas the administrator stood the countless traders and voyageurs who created the routes and built the forts of the fur trade; and

later the Royal Engineers who built the Cariboo Road.

The gold rush produced some striking figures such as Matthew Baillie Begbie, the judge who spent much of his life in the Cariboo proclaiming the law with panache and often with compassion. But behind Begbie stood his Irish chief of police Chartres Brew the constable without whom British Columbia would not have been saved from California-style vigilantism.

Billy Barker, the man who

struck it rich at Barkerville and lost it all to calculating women, was also significant. On my list he represents tens of thousands of anonymous miners who tramped out the pattern of our roads and drew farmers and ranchers to the province's northern regions.

BC's second premier, Amor De Cosmos, came from California with the Fraser River gold rush of 1858. He soon became British Columbia's first fighting journalist, its leading advocate of entry into confederation and later a stalwart defender of local interests. He combined the role of the first of our federalists with that of the first of our separatists, when as premier he threatened secession because Ottawa had not kept its word over completing the railroad in the agreed time.

De Cosmos established the populist trend in British Columbia. The most interesting politicians since that time have been populists. Most notably there has been W.A.C. Bennett who smashed the old-line political pattern in British Columbia when he led the Social Credit to power. The Socreds ruled, well or badly, because people trusted them in a highly polarized society of an arrogant class of exploiters and an increasingly militant mass of workers.

Inevitably the polarization has thrown up its rebels. Here I will cheat slightly by mentioning two figures together; one who became a hero among the Native people and another among radical labour. Simon Gun-an-Noot, the Gitskan outlaw who spent thirteen years in the bush avoiding the police, was later found innocent of murder. Ginger Goodwin, the labour militant who went on the run to protest conscription in the First World War, was shot down by the police on Vancouver Island.

Politics, even the extra-parliamentary kind, has not been the sum of British Columbian life. The province has been large and challenging enough for people to live most of their lives outside of the political context, partly in an increasingly active life of the arts.

It is from the arts that I draw two more names: Emily Carr, the first major artist to paint here, and Ethel Wilson, the first major artist to write in British Columbia. Both of these remarkable women must be regarded as representative of thousands of artists who continue to contribute to the cultural reality of British Columbia.

[1996]

Ten Women of BC

—⌒ CHARLES LILLARD

■ Charles Lillard, author and Pacific Northwest literary enthusiast, was a regular contributor to *BC BookWorld*. Selective in his scholarship and highly opinionated in his judgments, he had a deep respect for British Columbia literary culture and the characters who coloured it. In this essay he honours BC women, too often overlooked by official histories.

IN MY LAST COLUMN ("The shooting of Ginger Goodwin"), I went on at some length about BC's "character-rich past" but did not mention one woman. Not one. And much to my surprise not one woman phoned or wrote to set me straight.

Maybe it's because Emily Carr is the first female character to come to mind and maybe women, as well as men, are tired of hearing about her. As BC's sanctified misunderstood-genius, Emily Carr looms over us, fierce and otherworldly, much like the D'Sonoqua figure she has described in *Klee Wyck* (Clarke Irwin 1941).

Anyhow, it's likely that everything that can be said about Carr has already been said. But the same isn't true about many other remarkable women from BC history.

For many years Margaret "Ma" Murray was BC's reigning curmudgeon. She started her colourful journalism career in 1913 with the *Chinook* newspaper published in south Vancouver (unlisted in the Union Catalogue of British Columbia Newspapers) and continued with *The Bridge River Lillooet-News* (still publishing), the *Fort Nelson News*, the *Alaska Highway News* and *Country Life* magazine.

Ma is the central figure in Georgina Keddell's *The Newspapering Murrays* (1967) and Eric Nicol's popular play *Ma!* Not since the days of Amor de Cosmos and the *British Colonist* has such an independent voice as Ma's amused and challenged newspaper-reading public in BC.

Gwen Cash has been called "Canada's first female general reporter." Born in England in 1891, she began as a cub reporter with the *Vancouver Province* in 1917. She later married game warden Bruce Cash, a Manitoban, and they began fruit farming in Naramata. They later lived in Squamish and Sedro Woolley, Washington, before returning to BC.

Cash spent sixty-five years in Canada as a working journalist, tried her hand at turkey farming and worked in public relations for the Vancouver Board of Trade and the BC Teachers Federation. She died in Saanich at age ninety-two, the author of three books, including her memoir, *Off the Record* (1977).

Another name I half-expected to be reminded of was Mother Cecilia Mary, the Victoria nun who became world-renowned for her animal welfare activities after Big Jim Ryan photographed her with a dancing goat for *Life* magazine. Mother Cecilia continued her selfless work even after the Vatican commanded her to give it up. Although the late nun's legend continues to grow, there is only one book about her, E.D. Ward-Harris' *A Nun Goes to the Dogs* (Collins).

If some of these leading women were seen as "unladylike," certainly a much more feminine character was E. Pauline Johnson. "The Mohawk Princess," who was buried in Stanley Park in 1913, may still be Canada's best-known poet and storyteller.

Johnson's mixed-up love life, her Indian-White sensibilities and her life in what was then a largely male-dominated literary arena have been recounted in Betty Keller's biography *Pauline: A Biography of Pauline Johnson* (D&M), for which Keller received the Canadian Biography Award in 1982. Johnson's stories, *The Moccasin Maker*, originally published in 1913, was re-issued in 1987 by the University of Oklahoma Press.

Johnson's poems made Stanley Park's Lost Lagoon and Siwash Rock into lures for dreamers everywhere — whether critics liked her no-longer fashionable poetry or not ("The singing firs, and the dusk and — you").

No less romantic but much harder-headed, Mary Ellen Smith became the first woman to win a seat in the BC Legislature back in 1918. Two years later, Smith served as a minister without portfolio in Premier "Honest John" Oliver's cabinet, making her renowned and popular as the first Commonwealth woman to hold a cabinet position.

Writing under the pseudonym Minnie Smith, Mary Ellen Smith published *Is It Just?* (1910), probably the first Canadian novel to have divorce as its theme. The story is sentimental but not without its punch. Before the divorcee dies, "the last rays of the setting sun shone into the room, they rested upon the marble, and the smiling face of Mary Pierce, to whom the injustice of British Columbia law had caused such bitter suffering." Why no historical biographer has written about Mary Ellen Smith is a mystery.

Similarly, Jean Usher wrote *William Duncan of Metlakatla* and Margaret Poynter wrote *Miracle at Metlakatla*, but no female biographer has written about Marion (nee Goodwin) Collison, the first woman to live on the Queen Charlotte Islands and BC's north coast.

Collison lived on the Charlottes during the 1870s, giving birth to the first white child to be born there. If she isn't a remarkable "character" like the north coast's William Duncan, it's likely because no one has cared enough to do the necessary research.

The same is true in the case of Elizabeth Louisa Moresby, who most often wrote under the pen name of Lily Adams Beck, about whom next to nothing is known. She appeared in Victoria in 1919 and proceeded to write something in the neighbourhood of forty books by 1920. Many of these books were bestsellers, and one or two of them remained in print until the 1950s. One book, *The Treasure of Ho* was abridged by Barbara Carltand and reprinted in 1979. Quotes from Beck's *Story of Oriental Philosophy* still turn up now and again.

Beck was in her sixties when she started her writing career. She also used pseudonyms such as Louis Moresby and E. Barrington. The former is associated with Moresby Island in the Charlottes, named after Beck's grandfather, Sir Fairfax Moresby, a naval admiral. Mostly remembered today as an occultist, she was published by esteemed New York publishing houses.

"There is no weariness of mind in writing any of my books," she wrote, "I have learned from high Oriental thought that the body has its share in mental and spiritual training." Beck was famous for her seances and other activities only hinted at by elderly ladies in Victoria whose mothers once knew her.

Writer/artist Mildred Valley Thornton was as committed to coastal Indians as Emily Carr. And her handling of Native history and myths was much more sophisticated than Pauline Johnson's. Consequently, Thornton's *Indian Lives and Legends* (1966) has become a prized collector's item. But who remembers Mildred Thornton today?

Another forgotten BC writer is Alice Ravenhill, once a mover 'n' shaker in the women's institute movement and a pioneer in BC public health work. She wrote *Memoirs of an Educational Pioneer* (1951) and still reliable, though hard-to-locate, books on Indian art.

M. Wylie Blanchet wrote *The Curve of Time*, perhaps our best-loved book on coastal cruising. Only a "character" would have done what she did, and only a character could have survived. Frances E. Herring, whose many books about BC drift between fact and fiction, may have been BC's first woman writer of lasting importance.

Biographies of women such as Thornton, Ravenhill, Blanchet and Herring would give the words "BC characters" a much broader dimension.

Some years ago Margaret Ormsby, the dean of BC historians, said in an interview, "I think one reason our history is so interesting is that we have people with such strong personalities in our past. They're really individuals and they really stand out." Most "individuals" documented in our biographies, however, have been men. Ormsby made a noteworthy exception when she contributed her study of Susan Allison, *A Pioneer Gentlewoman of British Columbia* (1976), about one of the first female settlers in the BC interior.

[1990]

Dangerous Waters

—◦ MARK FORSYTHE

■ Ripple Rock near Campbell River took the lives of 114 mariners and claimed
125 vessels in just seventy-five years. In 1958 the largest non-atomic
explosion in history blasted Ripple Rock's lethal twin peaks to smithereens.
Hikers still trek above the narrows to gaze at the churning waters where
tides have screamed through at fifteen knots. The West Coast's deadliest
navigational hazard is naturally included in Keith Keller's compendium of
maritime stories, *Dangerous Waters* (Harbour), a gathering of twenty-one
accounts of peril and sometimes death, as outlined here by CBC Radio's
veteran host Mark Forsythe, an ongoing contributor to *BC BookWorld* for
more than a decade.

BRENT MELAN WAS ON A night run across Georgia Strait in 1990 with
his dad's fishing vessel *Lennie Jane* when a storm drifted further south
than forecasters had predicted. A huge wave flipped the vessel onto its
side. Melan had just enough time to send out a Mayday call and scramble
onto the overturned hull.

When he dove into the frigid water to retrieve the life raft, he couldn't get deep enough. Fearing he might become entangled in the lines, he put his clothes back on and held onto the hull for dear life.

"I prayed, I called on some dead people to help me. I didn't want to die and I knew I was close. I looked around for a piece of line to tie myself to the boat so at least they would have a body to bury."

At daybreak Tugboat Captain Dyke Noel spotted the overturned *Lennie Jane* and saved the grateful Brent Melan from dying of hypothermia. To this day Melan credits singing "You Are my Sunshine" — his girlfriend's favourite song — with keeping him focused on living.

Common threads run through these stories. There are several descriptions of adrenaline rushes that are somehow sustained for hours, helping stranded mariners to stay afloat or keep warm. Many survivors also describe being enveloped by a remarkable calmness that helped them to make the right decisions in desperate circumstances.

Fisherman Randy Morrison drifted in a survival suit for more than twenty-four hours in Hecate Strait. With his eyes swollen shut from the seawater, he imagined ghost boats coming to his rescue. Luckily the Canadian Coast Guard eventually fished him from the stormy seas.

Sometimes people make a priority of the oddest things. With his life in the balance, one fisherman remembered to pop two packs of his cigarettes into his pocket as his boat slipped underwater.

A powerful unwritten code also emerges: people tend to help one another even in the most horrific conditions. A father and son fishing at Nitinat Lake on the west side of Vancouver Island made the mistake of moving from the lake into open ocean following a storm. The standing waves in their path were unlike anything skipper Lauren Holman and his son Jason had ever experienced. The first roller sliced the cabin right off the boat. "I remember my boy saying, 'We're dead.' And that was only the beginning of the ordeal."

The waves were so powerful they continually smashed the two fishermen onto the ocean floor. Coming to the rescue, Tom Walton and his friend Ken MacDowell timed the intervals between the waves, managing to miraculously pluck the two men from the water as they went into shock.

The faint streak of a flare in Johnstone Strait once prompted logger Dan

Mooney to initiate a search, saving the lives of two American kayakers. In another case, a night-time flare sighting in Canadian waters put a US Coast Guard crew in the air over Juan de Fuca Strait from nearby Port Angeles, Washington. A shipwrecked man was lifted from a rock out-cropping by the American crew — with only five feet clearance between the chopper blades and adjacent cliff face.

We may not be able to agree on salmon quotas, but thankfully this longstanding agreement between nations to aid mariners in distress con-tinues to work. The skill of the Canadian Coast Guard is well docu-mented in these stories, including the action of lightkeepers frequently credited with initiating rescues and communicating vital information.

Coast Guard brass and federal politicians who've approved "de-staff-ing" and automation of the lights should be encouraged to read these accounts, and be reminded of those efforts.

[1998]

A Quiz: Know Thy Province

—© A.T.

The 900-page *Encyclopedia of British Columbia* has more than 4,000 entries from 200 contributors and each copy was originally distributed with an interactive CD-ROM version. Edited by Daniel Francis and published by Harbour Publishing, the *Encyclopedia* has more than 1,200 illustrations and took more than a decade to produce. As the most complete reference guide to all things British Columbian, the new Encyclopaedia offers a feeding frenzy for the curious, the scholarly, the journalistic, and the civic-minded. Go ahead. Test your knowledge. Anyone who scores 40-45 correct answers on this quiz is remarkable; anyone who scores more than 45 correct answers out of 50 has got to be cheating. Answers are provided at the end of the questions.

People
1. Who was dubbed "the next Marilyn Monroe"?
    a. Diana Krall
    b. Dorothy Stratten
    c. Pamela Anderson Lee

2. Who sang the bestselling Canadian single of all time?
   a. Bryan Adams
   b. Sarah McLachlan
   c. Terry Jacks

3. Who is Canada's leading bassoonist?
   a. Jon Kimura Parker
   b. George Zukerman
   c. Ben Heppner

4. Which outlaw is credited with inventing the expression "Hands up!"
   a. Frank James
   b. Frank Mclean
   c. Bill Miner

5. Who did Jack Kerouac call "the greatest poet living today"?
   a. George Bowering
   b. bill bissett
   c. Gerry Gilbert

6. Which environmentalist was assaulted and rammed by the French
   Navy when he protested nuclear testing in the South Pacific?
   a. Paul Watson
   b. Bob Hunter
   c. David McTaggart

7. Trick question: Who spent his teen years here?
   a. Atom Egoyan
   b. Brett Hull
   c. Earle Birney
   d. All of the above

8. Who, according to the *Globe & Mail* in 1999, was Canada's most
   famous living artist?
   a. Douglas Coupland
   b. Bill Reid
   c. Jeff Wall

Sports

9. Who was never a world champion?
   a. Jimmy McLarnin
   b. Daniel Igali
   c. Nancy Greene
   d. None of the above

10. Which athlete never won an Olympic gold?
    a. Karen Magnussen
    b. Elaine Tanner
    c. Harry Jerome
    d. All of the above

11. Who died from a self-inflicted gunshot wound?
    a. Sprinter Harry Jerome
    b. Sprinter Percy Williams
    c. Race Car Driver Greg Moore

History

12. Where is the oldest recorded human dwelling in British
    Columbia?
    a. Matsqui
    b. Port Clemens
    c. Invermere

13. What was the first widely used name for British Columbia?
    a. New Albion
    b. New Caledonia
    c. Queensland

14. Who resolved the 1859 Pig War between the US and Britain
    after an American settler shot a Hudson's Bay Company pig?
    a. A British monarch
    b. A German emperor
    c. A Spanish diplomat

15. What war in 1864 resulted in the hanging of five Tsilhqot'in men?
    a. Chilcotin War
    b. Cariboo War
    c. Colonial War

16. When did BC become a province?
    a. 1871
    b. 1881
    c. 1891

17. Where was the first wood pulp mill established?
    a. Swanson Bay
    b. Powell River
    c. Port Moody

18. Which group didn't have an island exclusively designated as a concentration camp for their group?
    a. Doukhobors
    b. Lepers
    c. Japanese Canadians

19. What modern group now uses the Imperial Palace mansion that was headquarters for the Ku Klux Klan?
    a. Vancouver Women's Club
    b. Canuck Place
    c. The Fraser Institute

Politics

20. Who was the first premier of British Columbia?
    a. Amor de Cosmos
    b. John Foster McCreight
    c. Matthew Begbie

21. Which provincial political party first campaigned for women to vote?
    a. Liberal
    b. Nationalist
    c. CCF

22. After W.A.C. Bennett, which premier had the longest term in office?
    a. John Oliver
    b. Richard McBride
    c. Bill Bennett

23. Which premier had the shortest term in office?
    a. Robert Beaven
    b. Joseph Martin
    c. Rita Johnson

24. When was the last time the Liberal Party won a provincial election, prior to Gordon Campbell?
    a. 1951
    b. 1946
    c. 1941

Geography

25. What is the longest river within BC?
    a. Fraser
    b. Columbia
    c. Skeena

26. After the man-made Williston Lake, what's the largest natural lake entirely in BC?
    a. Babine Lake
    b. Kootenay Lake
    c. Ootsa Lake

27. What is the highest mountain partially in BC?
    a. Mt. Fairweather
    b. Mt. Quincey
    c. Mt. Waddington

28. A tough one: In terms of their land mass in B.C., what is the largest mountain range?
    a. Central Plateau Mountains
    b. Coastal Mountains
    c. Rocky Mountains

29. A ridiculously tough one: what is the longest fjord?
    a. Gardner Canal
    b. Knight Inlet
    c. Portland Canal

Weather

30. What town has recorded the most rain in one day?
    a. Prince Rupert
    b. Ucluelet
    c. Bella Coola

31. Which city holds the Canadian record for longest string of rainy days in a row?
    a. Victoria
    b. Ucluelet
    c. Prince Rupert

32. Where was the largest recorded earthquake?
    a. Kootenays
    b. Queen Charlottes
    c. Pender Island

Flora & Fauna

33. Of the world's seventy species of abalone, which northern-most species is found here?
    a. Gastrapoda
    b. Phylum
    c. Pinto

34. The butterfly called Edith's Checkerspot is found nowhere else in the world but here:
    a. Similkameen Valley
    b. Chilcotin Valley
    c. Hornby Island

35. What is the most common shark species found on the BC coast?
    a. Dogfish
    b. San Jose shark
    c. Basking shark

36. What mammal doesn't appear on the BC list of Endangered Species?
    a. Lynx
    b. BC Lion
    c. Vancouver Island Marmot

37. Who is the Douglas Fir named after?
    a. James Douglas
    b. David Douglas
    c. Gilean Douglas

38. What's the official provincial tree?
    a. Red cedar
    b. Dogwood
    c. Sitka spruce

39. What is BC's floral emblem?
    a. Dogwood
    b. Salal
    c. Thunderbird rose

40. What's the provincial bird?
    a. Raven
    b. Steller's Jay
    c. Bald eagle

41. Which mythical creature is officially a protected species?
    a. Sasquatch
    b. Ogopogo
    c. Cadborosaurus

Miscellany

42. Who wrote a book set partially on the West Coast?
    a. Robert Louis Stevenson
    b. Jonathan Swift
    c. Jules Verne

43. What is the name of the most successful fishing lure developed here?
    a. Dolly's Varden
    b. Peetz Plum
    c. Buzz Bomb

44. After Vancouver, what's the most populous city?
    a. Victoria
    b. Burnaby
    c. Surrey

45. What corporation had the highest revenues in 1998?
    a. Westcoast Energy
    b. Jim Pattison Group
    c. MacBlo

46. Where is Canada's first underwater statue?
    a. Saltery Bay
    b. Vesuvius Bay
    c. Deep Cove

47. Which criminal prompted speculation and rumours about the size of his organ?
    a. Roger Ducharme
    b. Andy Bruce
    c. Robert Sommers

48. What Canadian export is exclusively from BC?
    a. Asbestos
    b. Molybdenum
    c. Cannabis sativa

49. In what year did the first shipment of seedless oranges arrive from Japan?
    a. 1884
    b. 1904
    c. 1924

50. What's the most famous BC photograph?
    a. The Last Spike
    b. Cariboo camel
    c. Miracle Mile
    d. Ripple Rock explosion

ANSWERS

People

1. a) Diana Krall of Nanaimo.
2. c) Terry Jacks' English version of Jaques Brel's *Seasons in the Sun* has sold more than 3 million copies.
3. b) George Zukerman came to BC in 1953 from Israel. Parker is a Burnaby-born pianist; Heppner is a world-renowned tenor from the Peace River district.
4. c) Bill Miner, the "gentleman" train robber, became a folk hero because he robbed the unpopular CPR. After BC film director Phillip Borsos made *The Grey Fox*, some historians have claimed Miner was a pederast.
5. b) bill bissett, born in Halifax, started blewointmentpress and has written more than 60 titles.
6. c) In 1972 and 1973 David McTaggart's courageous confrontations prompted France to discontinue its nuclear testing program, the last atmospheric tests in the world.
7. d) All of 'em. Brett Hull of North Vancouver was considered too lethargic to have a hockey career but joined the Penticton Knights junior team because management felt the son of Bobby Hull would help sell tickets. Born in Egypt, filmmaker Egoyan was mainly raised in Victoria. Birney moved from Alberta to Creston at age 12.

8. c) Born in Vancouver in 1946, Jeff Wall has gained an international reputation for his cibachrome photos of carefully constructed dramatic scenes.

Sports

9. d) Jimmy "Baby Face" McLarnin first won the world welterweight boxing championship in 1933; Nigerian-born wrestler Daniel Igali of SFU became the first Canadian to win gold at the world freestyle championships in 1999; Nancy Green (Raine), world skiing champ in 1968, was declared Canada's female athlete of the century.

10. d) Skater Magnussen was 1973 World Champion and Olympic silver medallist; swimmer Tanner set four world records and won two Olympic silver and one bronze medal; sprinter Jerome tied two world records and won an Olympic bronze medal.

11. b) Vancouver-born Percy Williams won two Olympic gold medals, set a world record for the 100-metre dash and shot himself in 1982.

History

12. a) Near Hatzic Rock in Matsqui, archaeologists have found evidence of human dwellings dating back 5,200 years.

13. b) Sir Francis Drake used the term New Albion; New Caledonia was more widely used until Queen Victoria chose the term British Columbia.

14. b) Germany's emperor arbitrated the dispute by placing the international border through Haro Strait. The American farmer received a small fine for shooting the pig but the US gained control of the San Juan Islands.

15. a) The BC government officially apologized to the Chilcotins in 1999. The Colonial War involved an attack by a British naval gunboat on an unfriendly Native village on Kuper Island in 1863.

16. a) Faced with the end of the gold rush and a growing public debt, British Columbians narrowly rejected joining the US and joined Confederation on July 20, 1871. The federal government took over the debt and agreed to complete a railway link within ten years.

17. a) Swanson Bay was a company town midway up the Inside
    Passage where the first pulp mill was built in 1909. By
    coincidence, the province's bestselling poet in the 1940s was
    Robert Swanson, the "Bard of the Woods," who was the
    inventor of air horns for trains.
18. c) Japanese Canadians were all detained inland. Piers Island in
    Haro Strait detained as many as 570 Doukhobors until 1935.
    D'Arcy Island, between 1891 and 1924, was used to detain lepers
    off the Saanich Peninsula. The leprosarium is featured in
    Marilyn Bowering's novel *To All Appearances a Lady*.
19. b) In 1927 the Klan claimed a provincial membership of 13,000.

Politics

20. b) McCreight, a bad-tempered and obstinate lawyer from
    Australia, was asked to serve as premier by Lt. Gov. Joseph
    Trutch. He held the office from November 14, 1871 until he
    resigned on December 23, 1872. He was a judge in New
    Westminster until he retired to England in 1897.
21. b) In 1894, BC's first labour political party sought women's
    suffrage, an end to property qualifications for candidates, a
    system of recall, the eight-hour workday and public ownership
    of banks, utilities and transport. Nationalist candidate Robert
    Macpherson, a carpenter, was elected to the BC Legislature in
    1894 and 1898.
22. b) Richard McBride (12); then Bennett (10) and Oliver (9).
23. b) Joseph Martin (3.5 months). Beaven (7.5 months); Johnson
    (7 months).
24. c) 1941.

Geography

25. a) Fraser River, 1399 km (Columbia 763 km within BC;
    Skeena 621 km).
26. a) Babine Lake (495 sq. km) easily beats out Kootenay Lake
    (407 sq. km) and Ootsa Lake (404 sq. km).

27. a) Mt. Fairweather (partially in Alaska) is 4,670 metres. Mt.
    Quincy Adams (also partially in Alaska) is 4,133 metres.
    Mt. Waddington, northeast of Knight Inlet, is 4,019 metres
    and completely in BC.
28. a) Central Plateau.
29. a) Gardner Canal at 114 km measures only one kilometre longer
    than Knight Inlet.

Weather

30. b) Ucluelet (489 mm).
31. a) It rained for 33 days straight in Victoria.
32. b) An earthquake off the coast of the Queen Charlottes in 1949
    measured 8.1 on the Richter scale.

Flora & Fauna

33. c) If you got this one, you're a good guesser.
34. c) Hornby. Equally difficult to spot is the metallic green damselfly
    found only in BC along a stream near Christina Lake.
35. a) Dogfish. (There haven't been any recorded shark attacks in BC.)
36. c) Lynx.
37. b) Scottish-born botanist David Douglas was hired as a collector in
    1823 by the Horticultural Society of London. For three years he
    ranged from his base at Fort Vancouver on the Columbia River.
    In his lifetime he introduced about 7,000 plants to England,
    more than any other person.
38. a) Red Cedar.
39. a) Easy the second time.
40. b) Steller's Jay became the provincial bird in 1987.
41. b) Ogopogo. The "demon" of Okanagan Lake emanates from
    tribal legends. Its English name is a palindrome from a music
    hall song performed in Vernon in 1926. A coastal equivalent,
    Cadborosaurus, was first sighted in 1933 in Cadboro Bay.
    There have been nearly 200 alleged encounters with "Caddy"
    (a serpent-like reptile, 15–20 metres in length, with a head
    resembling a horse) but Ogopogo gets the tourist industry hype.

Miscellany

42. b) Jonathan Swift's hero in *Gulliver's Travels* (1726) is caught in a fearful storm and sails up the northwest coast of North America to Brobdingnag, the land of the giants.

43. c) Buzz Bomb.

44. c) Surrey (304,477 pop.).

45. a) Westcoast Energy.

46. a) A bronze statue by Simon Morris was submerged 30 kilometres south of Powell River at Saltery Bay, a BC Ferry terminus.

47. a) Hanged for murder in 1950, Ducharme was a repeat sex offender with penile giantism.

48. b) Molybdenum is only mined at Endako, 170 km west of Prince George.

49. a) In 2000, Canada was still the largest export market for Japanese mandarin oranges in the world.

50. c) Roger Bannister passing John Landy at Empire Stadium in 1954 is one of the most famous photos in sports; it marks the first time two runners broke the four-minute mile barrier. The 1958

explosion of Ripple Rock near Campbell River was the world's largest non-nuclear peacetime explosion, CPR financial backer Donald Smith drove the last spike in the cross-Canada railway at Craigellachie, 45 km west of Revelstoke, in 1885. Two dozen camels were imported in 1962 from San Francisco as pack animals; the last one died in 1905.

[2000]

Holocaust & World War II

Prisoner #44070

_⌐ A.T.

■ Arguably, the most important author of British Columbia is not Pauline
Johnson, Douglas Coupland, William Gibson or Alice Munro. It's Rudolph
Vrba. As one of five people who ever escaped from Auschwitz, "Rudi" Vrba
was the main author of the first authoritative report on the true nature of the
concentration camps as well as the first reportage of mass murder to be
accepted as credible by the Allies. Little-known in British Columbia, Rudi
Vrba called Vancouver home for the last thirty-one years of his life.

IN CONVERSATION WITH me in 2001, Rudi Vrba described how he
and Alfred Wetzler became only the second and third persons to successfully escape from Auschwitz-Birkenau. On Passover Eve, April 7, 1944,
they hid inside a woodpile, in a previously prepared chamber, for three
days and nights, using kerosene-soaked tobacco spread around the woodpile to keep guard dogs from sniffing them out and alerting search parties.
The pair fled overland towards Slovakia after the SS cordon around the
camp was withdrawn on April 11.

After a perilous eleven-day journey, both men reached Bratislava in

Slovakia where they were taken into separate rooms at the headquarters of the Jewish community. They dictated separate reports that resulted in the Report on Auschwitz death camps, dated April 25th, 1944, in Zilina, Slovakia. This report became known in the historiography of the Holocaust as the "Vrba-Wetzler Report" or "Auschwitz Protocols." It describes the geography of the Auschwitz camp, the methodology of the gas chambers and a history of events in Auschwitz since April 1942.

(The first Auschwitz prisoner to escape, Siegfried Lederer, had fled on April 5, 1944, in the company of a Nazi corporal named Viktor Pestek who had fallen in love with a Jewish woman in the camp. Pestek was able to get a Nazi uniform for Lederer, who subsequently alerted Jews in the Theresienstadt ghetto in Czechoslovakia about how the Nazis were mass murdering Jews. Vrba and Wetzler escaped only six days after Lederer, so essentially they were alerting Jewish authorities around the same time, but Vrba and Wetzler had developed a system for corroborating their reports and so their estimates were harder to dismiss. The following month, two more Jews, Cslaw Morowitz and Arnost Rosin, escaped from Auschwitz on May 27, 1944.)

Having worked as slave labourers, sorting the belongings of gassed victims of the Holocaust, Vrba and Wetzler had been carefully counting the incoming trains between June 1942 and April 1944. As block registrars with relative freedom of movement, Vrba and Wetzler also had been able to observe preparations underway at Birkenau for the eradication of Europe's last remaining Jewish community, the eight hundred thousand Jews of Hungary. In their 32-page Vrba-Wetzler Report, they forewarned of Nazi preparations to kill those Hungarian Jews at the Birkenau compound. Vrba also chiefly wrote a report that was given to the Papal Nuncio in Slovakia, then forwarded to the Vatican. The Vrba-Wetzler Report II not only attempted to rationally estimate the scale of mass murder at Auschwitz, it also described methodology. As such, it's one of the most important documents of the 20th century. Copies are kept in the Franklin D. Roosevelt Library in New York, in the Vatican archives, and at the Yad Vashem memorial in Jerusalem.

By the end of June 1944, the Vrba-Wetzler Report had reached the governments of the Allies, but it was hardly soon enough. Estimates vary as to exactly how many prisoners were killed in the combined work camp/ death camp of Auschwitz-Birkenau, but it is clear there were more than in any other death camp. For the rest of his life, Vrba would claim that some Jewish leaders, most notably Hungarian-born Yisrael (Rudolph) Kastner (1906–1957), had failed to promptly and adequately alert the Jews of eastern Europe as to the dangers of extermination, thereby resulting in the deaths of thousands who might have been spared.

Vrba's reportage and expert witness testimonials from 1944 to 2006, when he died in Vancouver, made him one of the most essential individuals of the twentieth century. He was featured in numerous documentary films, most notably *Shoah* directed by Claude Lanzmann (Paris 1985), as well as *Genocide* (in the "World at War" series) directed by Jeremy Isaacs (BBC, London, 1973), *Auschwitz and the Allies* directed by Rex Bloomstein, in collaboration with Martin Gilbert (BBC, London, 1982) and *Witness to Auschwitz* directed by Robert Taylor (CBC, Toronto, 1990).

Vrba also appeared as a witness for various investigations and trials, such as the Frankfurt Auschwitz trial in 1964. In Canada he was called upon to provide testimony at the seven-week trial of Ontario's Ernst Zundel in 1985, when Zundel was found guilty of misleading the public as a Holocaust denier. In 2001 the Czech Republic's annual One World International Human Rights Film Festival established a film award in his name.

According to his curriculum vitae, Rudolf Vrba was born as Walter Rosenberg in Topolcany, Czechoslovakia, in 1924 as the son of Elias Rosenberg (owner of a steam sawmill in Jaklovce near Margecany in Slovakia), and Helena née Grunfeldova of Zbehy, Slovakia. At the age of fifteen he was excluded from the High School (Gymnasium) of Bratislava under the so-called "Slovak State's" version of the Nuremberg anti-Jewish laws. He worked as a labourer in Trnava until 1942. In March 1942 he was arrested for being Jewish, and on June 14, 1942, he was deported to the Maidanek concentration camp. He was transferred to Auschwitz on June 30, 1942.

As Prisoner # 44070 for almost two years, he mainly worked in Birkenau, in the so-called "Canada" warehouse where suitcases and other belongings of those taken away to the gas chambers were sorted. After escaping and contacting Jewish authorities, Walter Rosenberg joined the Czechoslovak Partisan Units in September of 1944 and adopted Rudolf Vrba as a nom de guerre. He fought until the end of the war in a unit commanded by Milan Uher ("Hero of the Slovak National Uprising in Memoriam") and was decorated with the Czechoslovak Medal for Bravery, the Order of Slovak National Insurrection and Order of Meritorious Fighter. He subsequently legalized his name, Rudolph Vrba, and became a citizen of Great Britain.

Vrba graduated in chemistry and biochemistry from the Prague Technical University in 1951 and obtained a post-graduate degree from the Czechoslovak Academy of Science in 1956. After five years of research at Charles University Medical School in Prague until 1958, he worked for two years as a biochemist at the Ministry of Agriculture in Israel. He then became a member of the Research Staff of the British Medical Research Council in London (1960–1967). When Vrba immigrated to Canada in 1967 and became Associate of the Medical Research Council of Canada, he began to use Rudi as his common first name. He worked for two years (1973–1975) in the United States as lecturer and research fellow at Harvard Medical School before joining the medical faculty at the University of British Columbia in 1976 as associate professor of pharmacology. Specializing in the chemistry of the brain, Vrba published more than fifty original scientific papers and also undertook research pertaining to cancer and diabetes.

Rudolf Vrba made a rare public appearance in Vancouver as a guest speaker at the 16th annual BC Book Prizes awards banquet in 2001. What became evident from his talk was that, quite simply, Rudi knew things on a host of subjects that other people didn't know. The last time I saw him, we met for coffee on West Broadway. He seemed fine, jovial, fatherly. We discussed our mutual friend, Stephen Vizinczey, and he left me with some parting advice: "Alan, whenever something bad happens, something upsetting or irritating, like locking your keys inside your car, or somebody steals your bicycle, stop yourself and ask, 'Am I going to remember this a year from now?' The anxiety will subside."

As an author, Vrba published a memoir, *I Cannot Forgive*, with Alan Bestic, in 1963, that has been translated worldwide. Significantly, the first

Hebrew edition of Vrba's memoirs was not published until 1988. He concludes his recollections by writing, "It is of evil to assent to evil actively or passively, as an instrument, as an observer, or as a victim. Under certain circumstances even ignorance is evil."

[2006]

Himmler's Scholars and the
Science of Delusion

―᮫ DAVID LESTER

■ In her fourth book, Heather Pringle, a science journalist with a masters
degree in English Literature, tells the story of Ahnenerbe — a Nazi "research
institute" founded by Heinrich Himmler, chief of the SS and architect of the
Nazi death camps. Here David Lester, designer of *BC BookWorld* since 1988,
reviews Pringle's *The Master Plan: Himmler's Scholars and the Holocaust*
(2006).

AS DEPICTED IN *Raiders of the Lost Ark*, Adolf Hitler's SS (*Schutzstaffel*
or Security Squad) was not only infamous for running the concentration
camps and gas chambers, and for serving as the Führer's bodyguards, the
world's most notorious police force also played a key role in unearthing
antiquities to ostensibly prove Aryan links to ancestral greatness.

   In 1935, Hitler sanctioned an obscure but powerful research arm of the
SS, the *Ahnenerbe* — a word meaning "ancestral heritage" — to uncover
ancestral treasures, to reconnect with past glories, and to present the Third
Reich as a model for fairness and middle-class decency. This Nazi think
tank recruited scholars to invent crackpot theories and to undertake ar-

chaeological digs around the world in order to authenticate Hitler's view of Aryans as a master race (tall, blonde and blue-eyed men and women who were the geniuses of civilization).

With extensive documentation, Heather Pringle's *The Master Plan: Himmler's Scholars and the Holocaust* (Viking) unravels the little-known story of the *Ahnenerbe*, a ridiculous but lethal construct that used bogus science to corroborate racism and justify the murder of six million Jews, intellectuals, gypsies (Roma) and homosexuals.

The dreamer and mover behind the *Ahnenerbe* was Heinrich Himmler. A thin, pale man who headed the SS, Himmler never exercised, and his head was too big for his body. He was nonetheless obsessed with Aryan perfection. It was Himmler who decided his SS men ought to look elegant in newly designed black uniforms from Hugo Boss, set off nicely by a silver death's head on their hats. This look, according to Himmler, would engender fear in men and "success with the girls."

Also an avid reader, Himmler maintained a list of his favourite books to recommend to others. If television had existed back in the 1930s, the exceedingly vain Himmler would likely have had his own interview program to showcase his favourite authors — the Nazi equivalent of the Oprah Book Club.

Himmler originally wanted *Ahnenerbe*-sponsored research to stimulate his SS men to learn more about Germanic folklore, religion and farming techniques, encouraging them to emulate the values of the Aryan race. Among their research projects were the following:

- In the 1930s, *Ahnenerbe* resurrected the debunked notion that measuring cranial features could effectively indicate intelligence and superiority. Nazi scholars hoped to discover racial data that might be useful in justifying the removal of all "mixed-races" from the Reich.

- In order to channel ancient knowledge, one of Himmler's scholars, Karl-Maria Wiligut, would go into trances. A violent alcoholic and ex-mental patient, Wiligut changed his name to Wisethor.

- Equally bogus, the prehistorian Herman Wirth claimed to have unearthed an ancient holy script that would help Germany resurrect its former greatness. Other notables were the classical scholar Franz

Altheim and his lover, the rock art researcher Erika Trautmann, who had turned down a proposal of marriage from Hermann Göring.

■ To explain the origins of the universe, Himmler and Hitler were particularly excited about the *Ahnenerbe*-sponsored "World Ice Theory." Its chief proponent, Hans Hörbiger, prided himself on never performing calculations and thought mathematics was "deceptive."

The Ahnenerbe's researchers plundered foreign museums, art galleries, churches and private homes, carting off valuable relics and masterworks of art. But with the onset of World War II, the activities of the *Ahnenerbe* became far more sinister:

■ The *Ahnenerbe* began using prisoners as guinea pigs to measure the effects of mustard gas and typhus.

■ When some SS members complained about the stress of shooting large numbers of women, children and babies in the Crimean, Himmler's henchmen in the *Ahnenerbe* ranks introduced mobile gassing wagons that could kill eighty people at once. With three mobile wagons in the Crimea, the SS was able to kill nearly 40,000 people, mainly Jews.

■ Human endurance at extremely high altitudes was tested using concentration-camp prisoners in a vacuum chamber, resulting in extreme suffering and many deaths. Painful sterilization experiments were also conducted on humans.

■ Himmler's "scientists" were also keen to know how long parachuting aviators could survive in freezing waters, and still be revived. Male prisoners were placed in ice cold tanks for hours and then laid on beds where naked female prisoners were instructed to warm them up and engage in sex.

Originally reliant on grants from a scientific and agricultural agency, *Ahnenerbe* also received financial help from corporate donors that included BMW. One of the organization's key sources of loot was Adolf Hitler's chauffeur. In 1936, when Nazi party member Anton Loibl wasn't driving the Führer to and from work, he was moonlighting as an inventor. One of his inventions was the shiny piece of glass now commonly mounted on bicycles to make them more visible at night.

When Himmler learned of Loibl's "bicycle reflector" innovation, he

Birkenau: Reliving a Nightmare

⌐ A.T.

■ Michel Mielnicki gets dizzy and nauseous when skin on barbecued chicken begins to curl and blacken over the coals. At age twelve, growing up as Mendel Mielnicki in Poland, he watched as a fellow Jew was assaulted and burned to death by two German soldiers. Ever since then, as a survivor of the Birkenau extermination camp, Mielnicki has carried the smell of incinerated Jews in his nostrils from the crematoria. Based on 800 pages of interviews, *Bialystok to Birkenau* is his horribly fascinating autobiography that recalls three-and-a-half years within the Nazi-run camps of Birkenau, Buna, Mittelbau-Dora and Bergen-Belsen. British historian Sir Martin Gilbert has provided a foreword for the autobiography. Mielnicki's story was told to, and edited by, John Munro.

MICHEL MIELNICKI WAS BORN in a small town near Bialystok in eastern Poland. The German army conquered the area in 1941, after which he survived fourteen months of privation and hunger in the Jewish ghetto of Pruzany, where Jews were terrorized by Poles and German soldiers alike. His family was then deported to Auschwitz in December 1942.

inked a deal to produce the new product. As head of the German police, Himmler was able to ensure the passing of a new traffic law that required all new German bicycles to have a reflector.

By 1942, Himmler was trapped in a frustrating marriage to a fifty-year-old. Wanting more children, he took his blond secretary, twelve years younger, as his mistress. She became ensconced in a mansion where he called her Little Bunny. When Gerda Bormann and her children dropped by for a visit, Little Bunny showed them a special room where a chair was made of human legs and feet. There was also a copy of *Mein Kampf* with a cover made from human skin. According to Pringle, even the children of Martin Bormann, a man known as the "zealous executor," were horrified.

In 1945, Hitler and Eva Braun committed suicide in their bunker beneath Berlin, and Heinrich Himmler fled, using an identification card that he stole from a police officer. After only a few weeks on the run as a member of the Nazi guerrilla movement called *Werwolf* (in English, Werewolf). Himmler devised a scheme to gain his freedom: he would offer his services to the occupying British and American forces, organizing *Werwolf* to fight against Communism. When this offer was rejected, Himmler swallowed a cyanide capsule during a medical examination and strip search.

Some of the *Ahnenerbe* scholars were arrested, tried, disgraced, executed or killed themselves, but others enjoyed highly-respected careers. In the last chapter, Heather Pringle tracks down ninety-year-old *Ahnenerbe* member Bruno Berger in a quiet German town. Berger, a so-called expert in racial studies, displayed emotion only when discussing the war-crimes trial he had endured, muttering about "how the law is biased." During several hours of conversation, he was unrepentant, believing that Jews should be regarded as a mongrel race.

The Master Plan is a restrained work of reportage, without proselytizing or exploitation, but on page 316, Pringle cites a 1971 survey that revealed fifty percent of the German population at that late date still believed that "National Socialism [Nazism] was fundamentally a good idea which was merely badly carried out."

[2006]

"Our wooden boxcar filled to capacity, its doors slammed shut and locked from the outside . . . the weeping, wailing, shouts and curses finally stilled. . . . We sat in stunned silence, hardly daring to think, lest we acknowledge what each of us knew to be true; we were about to be murdered by our German captors. And that particular moment, however long it actually lasted, was as good as this journey into hell was going to get.

"No one as yet had urinated in one of the corners, peed or shat in their pants, vomited all over him or herself or a neighbour, or died. . . . I did not know how long we'd been on the train when we finally reached the ramp at Auschwitz-Birkenau, and I do not know today . . . we ran out of food and water. It could have been three days. It could have been seven. . . . For sixteen or seventeen hours out of every twenty-four, it was so dark that you couldn't see your hand in front of your face. . . .

"Awakening was like a bad dream."

When the doors of the fetid transport were thrown open, the surviving Jews were driven out by whips and snarling German Alsatians. At the Auschwitz railway ramp, an immaculately dressed, cane-wielding *SS Unterscharführer* named Kühnemann mocked Mielnicki's father as a dirty Jew and began to beat him. His father was killed that day; his mother expired shortly after her arrival on a stretcher.

The 40-square-kilometre compound of Auschwitz was divided into three sections. In the concentration camp of Auschwitz I, prisoners wore striped uniforms but in the mass extermination camp of Auschwitz II, or Birkenau, workers like Mielnicki wore civilian clothes. In Auschwitz III, or Monowitz, Jewish and Slavic labourers in striped uniforms were contracted out by the SS to local factories.

Before Michel and his brother Aleksei were separated, they were tattooed on the outside of their left forearms, numbers 98039 and 98040 respectively. Because Aleksei was a beautiful singer, they received some preferential treatment from the sadistic Kühnemann, a music lover. After the war the psychopathic Kühnemann would enjoy a highly successful career in German opera under the assumed name of König.

Birkenau, says Mielnicki, was *the* death camp, not Auschwitz. When officials from the Red Cross came on inspection tours, they were shown Auschwitz, where there were clean clothes, bedding and even a brothel for gentile prisoners. Mielnicki lived by his wits under the five towering cremation-oven chimneys of Birkenau, forsaken by God but not luck.

"You could always tell when they were burning a transport of Jews from cities in the West," he says. "Flames shot high from the top of the chimneys, and hung over our heads, because they had more body fat than the half-starved Jews from the Polish ghettos. My people only produced a flat, yellow smoke. Not even sparks."

He ate grubs and cockroaches when he could catch them. He stole scraps of bread from the pockets of dead men. Life expectancy for workers was two or three months. Every day more prisoners threw themselves against the electrified fences. Memories of his mother's cooking gave Mielnicki the saliva necessary to chew bread that was at least 25 percent sawdust.

The foul-smelling latrines consisted of two hundred holes over a lake of human excrement. Just 20 feet away, Mielnicki saw two older prisoners murdered in a hideously original fashion "which really is saying something in a place like Birkenau." Two men were hoisted by their ankles and dropped headfirst through two holes, then held beneath the surface of the shit with long poles until the bubbles stopped.

Mielnicki was twice paraded naked before Auschwitz chief medical officer Josef Mengele, the "angel of death," but he wasn't selected to die. Mielnicki's frozen toe was cut off without anaesthetic but he avoided infection. He was transferred from Auschwitz and somehow rediscovered his faith.

As one of Himmler's slaves, he was a labourer at Buna, then at Mittelbau-Dora, where he was sentenced to be hanged in February 1945 for making a tin cup. He spent a week in four-by-six cage. "My mind has blotted out any despair I must have felt," he says. Due to an amnesty, he was punished instead with 25 lashes. Boney, less than one hundred pounds, he could hardly walk. "I think it is fair to say at this point I began to slowly lose my mind."

Once the Soviets began advancing, the Germans fled in fear. For a week the prisoners were denied all access to food or water by their machine guns-wielding Hungarian, Bosnian, Moslem and Croatian guards. "I remember there was shit everywhere. All over the floor. Dripping down from the bunks. . . . I was surrounded, in and outside my block, by ten thousand decaying corpses. People in my block were using them for pillows . . . there were billions of lice."

Mielnicki is frankly critical of the British liberation because some 13,000 prisoners at Bergen-Belsen didn't survive. "I don't think the British war cabinet or high command could have cared less," he claims. "We were a nuisance, an inconvenience, a drain on their resources. . . .

"I still think they could have saved many, if not most of the people who were dying in extreme misery from dysentery and typhus. Compare, if you like, what the Swedish medical team was able to achieve in the women's camp at Bergen-Belsen with the paltry British effort in the men's. . . .

"My God, initially they left the Hungarian SS guards in their watchtowers to prevent us from leaving that hellhole. And fed them better than they fed us. . . . I don't know anyone who doesn't wish that he or she had been liberated by the Soviets or the Americans."

(Coincidental with the publication of Mielnicki's memoir, a *Guardian* news story in July corroborated Mielnicki's viewpoint about British high command. Documents, newly declassified in the United States, confirmed that Winston Churchill's government knew about the Nazis' 1943 plans to seize 8,000 Jews in Rome for liquidation. Having received advanced information, neither Washington nor London gave Italian Jews any warning about their fate or made any international protest.)

"I have been a Holocaust witness ever since," says Mielnicki, age seventy-three, "which has been its own kind of hell."

Jews in Poland after the war were harshly treated by Poles; some were killed. As many as 100,000 Jews fled Poland, fearing for their lives. After waiting in vain for his brother to return to Bialystok, and concealing his Jewish identity to avoid being murdered, Mielnicki reunited with his sister Lenka in Prague and went to Paris.

At nineteen, he became Michel Mielnicki. Stateless and rootless, he married his Cracow-born wife, June, also a survivor of Nazi internment, in 1949. They immigrated to Montreal in 1953 where he became one of Canada's premier fur designers. Known at fashion shows as "Mister Michel," he became the principal fur designer for the Hudson's Bay Company, designing for royalty.

To enter Canada, Mielnicki, who now speaks seven languages, had taken the advice of a French-Canadian immigration officer; he denied his Jewish ancestry on his application form, pretending to be Russian-Orthodox. "I detected French-Canadian anti-Semitism long before anyone else," he says, "because I speak the language."

Disturbed by the political and racial climate in Quebec, Mielnicki and his wife came to Vancouver in 1966. They have two grown children, Alain and Vivian, and three grandchildren, and he has remained active in Holocaust education as a founding member of the Association of Former Concentration Camp Inmates.

■ ■ ■

In 1989, while visiting Germany, UBC Professor Rudy Vrba recognized SS Sergeant Kühnemann (aka König) performing onstage during an opera in Duisburg. As a Holocaust survivor, Vrba pressed a formal complaint with the German authorities. In 1990 Mielnicki went to Duisburg to testify against Kühnemann, the man who had killed his father. Among his other alleged crimes, Kühnemann was accused of ripping a baby from its mother's arms and smashing its head against a telephone pole. Mielnicki had no difficulty recognizing Kühnemann from a photo album of forty SS officers.

The case against Kühnemann, however, has dragged on for ten years. He remains free on the equivalent of $100,000 US bail. He is now too old, under German law, to be sent to prison. Mielnicki says he doesn't thirst for revenge so much as justice — recognition by the German state that Kühnemann is guilty of war crimes and murder.

"When I was liberated from Bergen-Belsen in 1945," he recalls, "I could not bring myself to join my colleagues in capturing and killing our former SS guards. I turned away when they were being beaten to death, saying that this was a matter for God, or for the law courts."

The disappointing Kühnemann trial has had one amazing and fortuitous outcome. The German prosecutor, having travelled to Auschwitz to glean evidence, discovered Aleksei Mielnicki had visited Auschwitz several months earlier to register for compensation. Michel's brother was living as a Soviet citizen in Ivano-Frankovsk, having survived the Mauthausen camp and been conscripted by the Soviet Army. The Mielnicki brothers met in Ukraine in 1992.

Michel Mielnicki's ordeal never ends. He still finds himself astounded and offended when he sees anyone throwing away anything edible. He can't escape Birkenau in his dreams, and the painful process of recalling his worst experiences for a book has been deeply depressing. Mielnicki says he has never been able to recover from the brutal death inflicted upon his father "by the forces of Hitlerian maleficence. . . . I still don't know how I didn't lose my mind."

Buried Lit: A German Childhood

⟿ A.T.

■ Never mind the typographical and spelling errors. Or the poor reproduction quality of the b&w photos. One of the most riveting memoirs you're not going to ever come across is Klaus G.M. Sturze's *From War to Peace: Memoirs of an Immigrant* (Penticton, Self-published), an account of surviving as a boy in post-war Germany. In this genre, Jerzy Kosinski's fictionalized *A Painted Bird* and "boy soldier" Ishmael Beah's *A Long Way Home* quickly come to mind, but both were skillfully embellished and/or edited, whereas Sturze's simply written account of his post-World War II privations is impossible to distrust.

"I WILL NEVER FORGET the night in January 1945," Klaus Sturze begins *From War to Peace*. "I wasn't yet ten years old. It was dark and bitter cold. We were standing on the platform for passenger trains in Breslau, Germany. Mother, her sister Lotte, whom we [had] been visiting, and I. Mother had suddenly decided we would go back to Schmuerckert, where we lived, a small town in Poland. A two-hour ride away. We found sheer pandemonium at the train station."

Sturze's mother is a resourceful woman who befriends many "uncles" to make it through the war. She miraculously gets the family to the Polish town only to learn the dreaded Russians are rapidly advancing. Either the Poles will kill them, or the Russian soldiers will rape his mother, so they join a phalanx of starving Germans, in horse-drawn carts, desperately trying to reach Berlin in the snows of January.

So begins a seamless nightmare — completely fascinating when safely viewed through the rear-view mirror of time. It is dedicated to all children surviving a war. Details have been burned into Sturze's mind. "The horror and the tragedies of the war were with us every day and still is hounding me fifty years later," he writes.

Initially we assume the mother is saving her child with heroic ingenuity. That is *his* perspective. She repeatedly outwits and overwhelms figures of authority, using either sex or anger, or both. But the truth is uglier. *From War to Peace* is doubling alluring as we grasp the narrator's emerging understanding of his manipulative mother.

"She never wanted me. She had told me this often enough, but she was not willing to give me up either. It was too much of an advantage to have a little kid around in times like this. I was to learn later on in life, as I had grown up, she had dumped me on my father when I was six weeks old and made off with another man. My father managed somehow to get my mother to live with him again when I was three years old."

Evil begets evil. His mother has repeatedly used him to gain money and sympathy from her many lovers (including SS officers during the war). When he reaches his teens and earns money as an apprentice in a hotel, his mother steals money from him. With half the city in ruins, at age fifteen, Sturze asserts his independence, escaping from her tyranny.

In the mid-1950s, newly married, Sturze hopes to immigrate to Canada with his new wife and daughter. Estranged from his mother, he meets her in a café and asks for a loan. She replies, "Do you think I'm stupid? I'll never see my money again. No way. You got a good looking wife. She can go and make some pussy money." Appalled, Klaus calls her the dirtiest human he has ever come across. It was the last time he ever spoke to her. "Even her cries for me on her deathbed could not move me to see her. I had no feelings for her. She didn't exist for me."

Conversely, Sturze's simple descriptions of his sexual awakenings as a boy and teenager are touchingly candid, sensitive and deeply appreciative of women. This strange friction between his loathing for his mother and his admiration for female contact lends a necessary poignancy — we are on his side, we accept him as an individual storyteller beyond his platform as a victim of war. Every time he recounts an episode about the dawning of sexual relations, it serves as a beautifully rendered oasis within the narrative, a jarring reprieve, a detour towards health.

Evidently intense cruelty and privation can magnify beauty and joy. Similarly, the strength of the author's affection for Canada as a haven in which he has thrived is likely derived from the depth of his bitter resentment of Nazi Germany and Soviet-occupied Germany.

There is an inelegant afterword that any commercial publishing house would likely expunge or sanitize. Under the word Epilog [sic], we learn: "Looking back today, I think the Nürnberg [Nuremberg] trial missed its mark. The maniacal and unconscionable leadership of the Nazi government should not have been hung, even though they deserved it. The death penalty was way too good for them. It was all over within a second.

"There was no suffering. The terror and the slaughter, caused by them, to humans of all nation[s] involved, was horrendous. I think they should have been sentenced to life in prison at hard labour and received every Sunday five lashes with the whip, until they died in prison. All of the inner government were guilty, because they all saw the slaughter and no one was willing to put an end to it."

There are thousands of heartfelt and necessary first-person testimonies by Jews and others who suffered under the Nazis, and who lost their loved ones to atrocities and other police-state machinations; Sturze's perspective as an innocent German child is alarming in its own way. Here is the collateral damage of despotism and racism. From an historical perspective, this is second-class horror, but not for the individuals who absorbed it.

The perpetrators of evil didn't suffer; the child in Klaus Sturze did. He is angry about it, and haunted by that injustice. *From War to Peace* is the mirror image of a real life, an act of truthfulness, so unfettered by pretension that it is artful. It was self-published in 2007. There is no distributor, no professional representation. In March of 2010, there was only one copy for sale on the internet, from a store in Cranbrook. The author lives in Penticton. There was no listing on AbeBooks.com. You can almost not buy it. And you can't invent it.

It exists beneath the rubble of commerce and creative writing.

[2010]

More Holocaust Literature from BC

⌐ JOAN GIVNER & A.T.

■ Barbara Ruth Bluman's *I Have My Mother's Eyes: A Holocaust Memoir across Generations* is the fourth volume in a series of survivors' narratives published by Ronsdale Press in conjunction with the Vancouver Holocaust Education Centre. Each of these books brings to light previously under-reported incidents. This series prompted this introduction to nine additional books related to the Holocaust from British Columbia authors.

I HAVE MY MOTHER'S EYES: A Holocaust Memoir across Generations by Barbara Ruth Bluman begins long before the outbreak of war. As the daughter of a successful businessman, Zosia Hoffenberg led a comfortable life in Warsaw and fell in love with eighteen-year-old Natek Bluman.

While learning business skills in New York, Natek heard US media reports and understood the enormity of the threat to European Jews, but when Natek returned to Poland, Zosia's father dismissed his warnings.

Three months after the German bombs fell on Warsaw, Zosia joined Natek in the countryside. There they were married and embarked on a long journey to freedom. Through Natek's resourcefulness they managed to reach Lithuania, where they obtained visas allowing them to travel by rail across Russia, then sail from Vladivostok to Japan.

Perhaps most significantly, in *I Have My Mother's Eyes* we learn of Chiune Sugihara, the Japanese Consul in Kaunas, Lithuania, whose courage allowed the Blumans to escape. On July 26, 1940, Sugihara woke to see a crowd outside his consulate clamouring for exit visas. They were desperate people who knew they would be murdered when the Germans invaded Lithuania.

Acting in defiance of direct instructions from the Japanese Foreign Ministry, and fully aware of the danger to his own family, Sugihara went ahead and issued the visas. In doing so, he saved the lives of between six and ten thousand Jews. Sugihara is honoured with others of the "Righteous among the Nations" at Yad Vashem.

On June 26, 1941, the Blumans sailed from Yokohama on an aging freighter, the *Hie Maru*, for Vancouver — completing a journey of almost two years. A year later, Natek enlisted in the Canadian army, telling his pregnant wife, "I will never forgive myself if I don't fight against the Nazis."

Zosia's daughter, Barbara Ruth Bluman, a distinguished Vancouver lawyer committed to human rights, was in the last stages of cancer when she set down her mother's story, interweaving it with her own. An afterword was written, in turn, by Barbara's daughter, Danielle Schroeder, following the deaths of both Zosia and Barbara, making this a three-generational family project.

■   ■   ■

Born Leon Kaganowicz in Eisiskes, Poland, in 1925, Leon Kahn grew up in a *shtetl*, or village, and lived through first the Russian and then the German invasion. He tells how, at sixteen years of age, he returned from an excursion to his village and, from the edge of a gravel pit, witnessed the mass murder of the community's women and children, the women being repeatedly raped before being shot. He then took to the forest and joined the partisans in order to carry out raids on German targets. He survived Nazi search parties, Jew-hating Soviet, Polish and Ukrainian partisans and outdoor hardships to emerge at the war's end, along with thousands of Jews, from the forests.

He explains how the Nazis began by not allowing his people to walk on the sidewalks; they could only walk in the gutters. Belongings were confiscated, yellow Stars of David had to be worn. Most of his village's 5,000 people were eventually killed. Kahn gave his life meaning by fighting back, but at war's end both Russian and American forces detained Kahn until they could verify that he was not an enemy alien.

He survived and immigrated to Vancouver in 1948, where he worked successfully in real estate, and died in 2003. *No Time to Mourn: The True Story of a Jewish Partisan Fighter* (Ronsdale) was written after he had become a well-known philanthropist and businessman. Kahn's account is dedicated to his 24 close relatives (including his mother, father, sister, brother and grandmother) who were killed by the Nazis.

■   ■   ■

In Rhodea Shandler's *A Long Labour: A Dutch Mother's Holocaust Memoir* (Ronsdale) the scene shifts from Poland to Holland. Shandler went into hiding on a farm, giving birth to a daughter in a frigid pigsty in December. Her child was whisked away by the Resistance and raised in the safety of a Gentile household. Lillian Kremer, an expert on the Dutch Holocaust, contributed a preface to Rhodea Shandler's story. Such prefaces are important because the subjects raised in this series are often contentious ones.

For instance, the recent release of the movie *Defiance*, while it focuses attention on the Jewish partisans, has generated a flurry of controversy. A headline in a Polish newspaper questions whether the partisans were heroes or murderers. The British journalist, Anne Karpf, the daughter of a Holocaust survivor, criticized the movie for depicting the partisans in combat with the Nazis when, in her opinion, they avoided confrontation and merely tried to stay alive.

The subject of righteous Gentiles is also a contentious one. The debate is dramatized within this series by the contrasting opinions of two of the contributors. Leon Kahn, for example, makes a broad indictment of those who did nothing: "I believe it is absolutely imperative to mention the responsibility of the Roman Catholic Church and its clergy for their part in the wholesale and unprecedented slaughter of Central Eastern European Jewry. They were well aware of the daily horrors inflicted on Jews by their devout Catholic parishioners. Yet not once did Rome or any of its deputies throughout Eastern Europe raise a voice in protest."

On the other hand, Sir Martin Gilbert's definitive *The Righteous: The Unsung Heroes of the Holocaust* contains a broadly inclusive catalogue. He praises members of the clergy, including the Catholic Church and Pope Pius XII, for their efforts in saving Jews.

■ ■ ■

Born in Warsaw, Lillian Boraks-Nemetz escaped while still a young girl from the Warsaw Ghetto and lived in Polish villages under a false identity. Boraks-Nemetz is best-known as the author of young adult novels that include *The Old Brown Suitcase*, a fictionalized account (based on her own experience) of a 14-year-old immigrant girl, Slava, who comes to Canada from Poland after World War II. Her suitcase is filled with memories of the Warsaw Ghetto where she left behind her parents and sister.

The girl's problems of adjustment to her new life in Canada as a teen-aged immigrant Jew are juxtaposed with her heart-wrenching memories of her lost childhood in Poland. *The Old Brown Suitcase* won the Sheila A. Egoff Prize, among other awards. Other novels in her Slava trilogy are *The Sunflower Diary* (Roussan, 1999) and *The Lenski File* (Roussan, 2000).

■ ■ ■

Born in Krakow in 1945, Eva Wydra (later Eva Hoffman) moved from Poland to Vancouver with her Jewish parents at age thirteen. She describes it as the formative experience of her life.

"The assumption was that we would never go back," she says. "There was a great deal of a sense of rupture about it. The differences between Krakow and Vancouver were enormous. There was a cultural trauma, let us say, during those first stages of immigration."

As the daughter of survivors (not camp or forest survivors), she studied at Yale and received her PhD in literature from Harvard. *Lost in Transla-tion: A Life in a New Language* (1989) describes her experiences in Poland and Vancouver.

■ ■ ■

Irene Watts has won three Canadian Jewish Book Awards. *Good-Bye Marianne: The Graphic Novel* (Tundra), illustrated by Kathryn Shoemaker, is her poignant story about the *Kindertransport* that saved ten thousand Jewish children in Germany prior to the outbreak of World War II.

Watts' original print version, about an eleven-year-old named Mari-anne Kohn in 1938, won the Geoffrey Bilson Award for Historical Fiction and the Isaac Frischwasser Memorial Award for Young Adult Fiction.

■ ■ ■

Rhoda Kaellis gathered the experiences of fifteen Holocaust survivors over a period of nine months for the fictional story of twelve-year-old Sarah Carozo, the only child of a Jewish family in post-World War II New York City, and Lilly, her Belgian cousin who comes to live with her after her parents have died in a concentration camp. Her book *The Last Enemy* (Arsenal Pulp, 1989) was conceived after Rabbi Victor Reinstein of the congregation Temple Emanu-El in Victoria suggested recording recollections of the Holocaust in 1987.

■ ■ ■

Helene Moszkiewiez worked within the Belgian Resistance and main-tained three identities, Jewish, Belgian and German, while working for two years as a clerk in Gestapo headquarters in Brussels. The Germans took control of Belgium when she was nineteen. "They were so stupid," she told Geoffrey Molyneux of *The Province* in 1985. "They thought only in caricatures. You know, the Jewish man with a long black beard and a large hooked nose. Many of the Gestapo were the dregs. They were just there because they were cruel. The *Abwehr* intelligence men, now they were bright and you had to be careful when they were around."

While residing in West Vancouver, she wrote her memoirs, *Inside the Gestapo: A Jewish Woman's Secret War* (Macmillan, 1985). Her story recalls creating false identity papers, helping POWs escape, working within the Gestapo, hearing screams of SS victims, stealing information to rescue Jews scheduled for transport, and killing a Gestapo officer. "We heard about the camps from the BBC," she recalled, "but so many Jews seemed to think it couldn't happen to them. You know, it could happen again. Jews have to be ready to fight."

■ ■ ■

As a social worker in the psychiatric department of Montreal's Jewish General Hospital, Fraidie Martz met some of the 1,123 Jewish war orphans whom the Canadian government reluctantly allowed into Canada from 1947 to 1949. Her non-fiction account, *Open Your Hearts* (Vehicule, 1996), recalls how and why these war orphans were brought to Canada. It received the Joseph and Faye Tannenbaum Award for Canadian Jewish History in 1997.

■ ■ ■

Born in Budapest, Hungary, in 1920, Steve Floris survived the Holocaust and was later reunited with his pre-war love, Eva. They escaped Soviet-occupied Hungary and went to Austria, where they worked in UN refugee camps before immigrating to Canada. They owned and operated the Ferguson Point Tea House for many years. His *Escape from Pannonia* (Granville Island Publishing, 2002) recalls their lives together.

[2009]

Portrait of the Artist
as a Listener

—◌ KRISTIN BOMBA

■ Weighing in with 312 pages of meticulous original art, David Lester's
The Listener (Arbeiter Ring) is a graphic novel that manages to combine
the rise of Hitler with a contemporary woman's search for meaning in the
great art of Europe.

DAVID LESTER'S *The Listener*, on its historical and political level, revisits
how Adolf Hitler was one of the original spin doctors, turning his party's
narrow electoral victory in the state of Lippe, in 1933, into an alleged
"massive victory" that enabled him to be appointed chancellor of Germany, by President Hindenburg, just two weeks later.

On an intimate and personal level, Louise — the listener of the title
— takes a sabbatical tour of the museums of Europe, trying to overcome
guilt and sadness after a young activist, inspired by one of Louise's sculptures, fell to his death while hanging a protest banner off the Woodward's
"W" tower in Vancouver. She receives letters blaming her for the death
of the activist.

As an antidote, Louise re-explores famous and favourite paintings and sculptures throughout Europe. The politics behind these works of art swim in her mind. Along the way, she meets various people who affect her life.

In Austria, she meets Tomas, a man interested in the people behind the works of art, specifically destructive people who were artists or poets (Hitler was a painter; Stalin and Mao were poets). Tomas and Louise visit a concentration camp where Louise struggles to absorb the atmosphere, but she feels unable to comprehend the magnitude of what occurred there. As they journey through Europe, they discuss how they became artists, and what inspires them.

They discuss the nature of the art (Do people see what they're meant to see, learn what they're meant to learn, or see what they already understand?) and the possible obligations of artists to the world. Of particular note is a story about Orson Welles who was once asked to run for the senate and declined, whereupon Joseph McCarthy won that election.

The rise of Hitler is told through the memories of an older couple that Louise meets, Marie and Rudolph. In flashback scenes, Marie and Rudolph recall working for a newspaper in the conservative state of Lippe, in Germany, in the 1930s. Louise listens as the couple recall joining the DNVP (German National People's Party), hoping for the return of the monarchy in Germany. The world slowly begins to change around them, and the Nazi party grows, along with attacks on Jewish people.

A crisis in the federal government is approaching as Hindenburg dithers in selecting a new chancellor of Germany. The top picks are DNVP's Alfred Hugenberg (who owns the paper where Marie and Rudolph work) and Adolf Hitler.

Along comes the state election in Lippe. Prior to this election call in Lippe, the Nazi Party was losing its appeal. Hitler's stubborn desire to hold all the power in his hands, or none at all, was hurting the party. But Hugenberg chose to strike a deal with Hitler, under the guise of national unity, hoping for a position of power in a Hitler-led government.

This compromise of principles by Hugenberg has disastrous consequences almost immediately. First, Marie and Rudolph's newspaper is ordered by Hugenberg to cease attacks on the Nazi Party. Hitler's party is in deep financial trouble and the Lippe election fight may be his last.

The Nazi party throws everything they have into the campaign. His storm troopers arrive from across Germany, converging on Lippe. DNVP campaign posters are covered over with Nazi posters. Local rallies are manipulated, and members of the opposition are brutally attacked at their own rallies.

Newspapers backed by the Nazis spread their propaganda while the DNVP silences its own papers and reporters, shuts down its rallies, and allows the Nazis to dominate the campaign without protest. The Orson Welles anecdote, as previously mentioned, now takes on greater significance to the reader.

The Nazis won the Lippe election in January of 1933 with only 39 percent of the vote. They had increased their vote count by only 4,000 votes from a preceding federal vote that was held in Lippe only three months earlier, in November.

After Hitler was subsequently appointed to serve as chancellor, other political parties were banned. The DNVP was dissolved, opposition leaders were found dead, citizens suspected of being Jewish or communist were beaten, and persecution of the Jews was escalated. That narrow victory in Lippe became an annual celebration in which Hitler skillfully presented himself as Germany's hero.

Marie and Rudy express their regrets for not having done more, and Louise returns home with their memories and a special gift. Back home, Louise is even more lost than before, and slips back into her previous lifestyle, returning to the man she had broken up with.

After several months, a man named Walter appears. He's an acquaintance of the Cambodian-born activist named Vann, who plunged to his death near the outset of the story. This time Louise listens as Walter tells her the life story of Vann, a Cambodian doctor who survived genocide under the Pol Pot regime. Vann lost his parents and was never able to overcome his survivor's guilt. Because the Pol Pot regime targeted particular artists for execution, Vann took a great interest in art, wondering what made artists so dangerous that so many had had to die.

Rather than blaming Louise for Vann's death, Walter has come to tell her that Vann was inspired by her work. Walter reassures Louise that Vann was solely responsible for his own death. Louise is moved by the story and takes solace from Walter's absolution of her culpability.

As far-right-wing activities are again coming to the fore at the outset of the twenty-first century in Germany, including anti-Semitic activity and violent confrontations, Louise is inspired to create a new sculpture that is the culmination of all she has learned on her journey through Europe, and all her "listenings."

Louise is more comfortable expressing and explaining herself through drawing than talk. If I can include myself here, then I'm much the same with the written word. She is more of a listener, an observer, absorbing everything around her, and I found I could easily relate to her. I could sympathize with the way she runs from her guilt, even as it chases her every step of the way, until she is finally able to absorb Vann's actions and create her masterpiece.

The stereotypical artist is a "beautiful soul" putting passionate feelings to canvas, print, stone, or song. It's not often that artists are presented as mass murderers or power hungry dictators. But one of Hitler's greatest regrets is that he was never able to build a museum to house his personal collection of art.

It's depressing to think that someone who enjoys expression and creation could so love destruction. For myself, I prefer to write Hitler off as nothing more than a delusional, paranoid psychopath, someone who saw himself as Germany's new Siegfried, the Motherland's hero come to destroy the Nibelungs — the Jews.

But it's impossible to deny his artistic "flair," or the way in which he and his party so skillfully manoeuvred a victory. Lester inserts several images and quotations of the propaganda used by the Nazis. The xenophobia is rampant. The vitriol is truly horrific and saddening. Such propaganda ignited an entire nation and motivated the murder of millions.

For anyone interested in serious questioning of the role of art in society, *The Listener* is rich with quotations on the subject and Lester uses many excellent quotes as chapter headings. At first I thought, hey, real people don't talk like that. But people who live deeply in art probably do. Artists aren't exactly "normal." So *The Listener* reveals that when you live and breathe art on a daily basis, it becomes a central part of your life even outside its most practical uses.

So *The Listener* is a good story for people familiar with artists and art movements. Lester deftly slips these things, their history, their impact, into conversations between his characters, and ingrains them into their lives. As for Lester's art, it sweeps across the pages, changing as if it is alive with his thoughts.

This is far from a traditional comic book. It doubles as an intriguing read for anyone with an abiding interest in the psychology of Hitler and the propaganda machine that was the Nazi Party. *The Listener* is not something you can flip through in an afternoon. I spent hours going through the book, taking notes, forming thoughts.

Much of the dialogue from Hitler (and other Nazi party leaders) contains direct quotes from his speeches and writings. Lester details what is historical fact and what is his own invention in the back of the book, which also includes an excellent timeline of the rise and fall of the Nazi party.

Another important inclusion is a collection of small biographies of several Nazi or pro-Nazi animators, filmmakers, and cartoonists, detailing their specific involvement in the Nazi propaganda machine, and their lives after the fall of the Third Reich.

[2011]

SECTION 4

Writing in BC

Famous Literary Visitors

─ A.T.

■ A Special Issue of *BC BookWorld* devoted to famous literary visitors began
  with Michael Buckley describing the mysterious story of Lobsang Rampa,
  followed by staff articles on more than 25 other famous visitors.

T. Lobsang Rampa

It is a little-known fact that sometime in the early 1970s, T. Lobsang
Rampa and his entourage lodged for about two years at the Denman Place
Inn (as it was then known) in Vancouver's West End. The upper floors
hosted residential suites with expansive views over English Bay. The self-
designated guru stayed close to the top of the 35-storey building where he
led a hermit-like existence, making occasional wheelchair forays to Denman Place Mall. It's possible he composed one or two books during his
stay. He usually wrote in bed, closely monitored by his Siamese cats.

Lobsang Rampa had launched one of the greatest literary hoaxes of the
twentieth century with the publication of *The Third Eye* in 1956. He fled
from scrutiny to hide out in British Columbia and Alberta. This bestselling
author of esoteric bafflegab, Lobsang Rampa, once wrote about his travels

by flying saucer from Tibet to a paradise on Venus — but he never mentioned his two-year stay in Vancouver.

Lobsang Rampa (not his real name) was a refugee of the celebrity kind, on the run from news hounds. While he revelled in the attention he received from his books, he hated to be recognized in person. That's likely because he built his reputation under the persona of a Tibetan lama-physician purporting to be the author of a tome called *The Third Eye*. The first-person narrator is a Tibetan physician with the psychic ability to read human auras — via a third eye sited vertically in his forehead.

Rather than present *The Third Eye* as fiction, Rampa stuck to his Tibetan lama identity like Velcro — in the interest of generating greater sales figures. The ruse worked, with Rampa laughing all the way to the bank by writing more books about his travels in Tibet and other exotic realms. His books developed a huge cult following, selling in the millions — by one count, over five million; by another count, over twelve million to date.

In person, however, the illusion didn't quite hold up. Rampa did not look even remotely Tibetan, and he spoke not a word of the language. There were a number of Tibetologists in London who were keen to expose this charlatan by reminiscing about their time in Tibet. Among them was Heinrich Harrer, author of *Seven Years in Tibet*, and fluent in the Tibetan language.

Rampa was not so keen to meet the Tibetologists. The curious were informed that he was either seriously ill, or on a lengthy meditation retreat — and could not be disturbed. A news story eventually broke revealing Rampa as Cyril Henry Hoskin, the unemployed son of a plumber from Devonshire.

Rampa weaseled his way out of monstrous contradictions in a later book by claiming that his English body had been "possessed" by the spirit of a Tibetan lama. That happened on a Tuesday, when he fell out of a tree, thus explaining his full *nom de plume*: Tuesday Lobsang Rampa (wisely abbreviated as T. Lobsang Rampa in his works).

When news of Rampa's real identity came to light, the Rampas promptly decamped from London to a fort-like structure on the coast of Ireland, overlooking the sea. They were under virtual siege from members of the press, who tried to spy over the walls through periscopes and went through their garbage.

Fed up with this kind of attention, the Rampa entourage flew to the east of Canada, spending some time roving around Ontario, Quebec and the Maritimes. Then they decided to shift to the west coast.

At the helm of the Rampa entourage was haughty Sarah Rampa, his wife — a former nurse who handled both business and Rampa's frail health. In the role of companion and secretary was Sheelagh Rouse, a pretty young woman who came aboard in Ireland — on the lam from a marriage that didn't work out (there was some speculation in the press of the day about whether her involvement was more than secretarial). And there were several Siamese cats, which the Rampas doted on, preferring feline company to human. This had side benefits. According to Rampa, his Siamese cat Fifi Greywhiskers telepathically dictated an entire book to him, which he diligently translated from the "Siamese cat language" into English. The book is called *Living with the Lama*.

It is through the eyes of Sheelagh Rouse that Rampa's Vancouver interlude comes into focus — described three decades later in a book called *Twenty-Five Years with T. Lobsang Rampa* (Lulu Books, 2005). According to her, Rampa liked the water views in Vancouver, but he found the people less than friendly, and definitely not cat-friendly (the entourage failed to find a suitable rental apartment that would accept cats).

By the 1970s, Rampa was suffering from chronic health problems and was getting around in a wheelchair. He railed against Vancouver's lack of wheelchair access, and against 'women's libbers' and teenagers. But the last straw was fans chasing him along the streets of the West End (he pretended not to be Dr. Rampa when accosted).

Eventually, the Rampas moved to Calgary, where they were left in peace for a lengthy stretch of time — over six years. Rampa even dedicated a book to the city of Calgary. In 1980, Sheelagh Rouse had a falling-out with Rampa over his egocentricity and bizarre behaviour, and left in a huff — taking up employment in Vancouver. Rampa promptly disowned her. Rampa died in Calgary in 1981. His lucrative royalties were apparently donated to several cat organizations in Canada and the US.

Death usually puts a crimp in the output of most authors. Not so

Lobsang Rampa. His books continue to sell and sell, with *The Third Eye* remaining his most popular title. He even managed to produce a book posthumously. It is called *My Visit to Agharta*, about his foray to the subterranean Himalayan realm of Agharta. The book was cobbled together from supposedly long-lost papers belonging to Rampa, and published in 2003 — over ten years after his death. To this day, librarians are mystified over where to shelve Rampa's books — under religion, occult, paranormal, thriller, sci-fi or autobiography. The best solution yet seen: file them under "New Age."

Allen Ginsberg

Allen Ginsberg made several visits to Vancouver, notably in November of 1978 when he headlined two evenings in support of his friend Warren Tallman's Vancouver Poetry Centre and its "defence" of Talonbooks under attack from Conservative MPs in the House of Commons.

The former advertising scribe and author of *Howl* in the 1950s asked for a "good vibe" audience for "lifting the city to Heaven which exists and is everywhere about us." When Ginsberg appeared at the PNE Gardens Auditorium, the tone-deaf poet received guitar backup from Gary Kramer of the venerable Vancouver group Brain Damage. While in Vancouver, Ginsberg expressed some dismay that his droning and simple harmonium playing were not met with a recording contract from Columbia. Ginsberg, who died in 1997, never made it onto *American Idol*.

Raymond Chandler

When the United States joined the First World War effort, mystery novelist Raymond Chandler enlisted in the Canadian forces and underwent basic training in Victoria with the Gordon Highlanders prior to being sent to France via Halifax. Although he was born in Chicago, Chandler had been raised in England where he became a naturalized British citizen.

Chandler once recalled his three-month stint in Victoria in a letter to a friend: "If I called Victoria dull [in a preceding letter], it was in my time dullish as an English town would be on a Sunday, everything shut up, churchy atmosphere and so on. I did not mean to call the people dull. Knew some very nice ones."

Later to become widely known for his novels *The Big Sleep* (1939),

Farewell, My Lovely (1940) and *The Long Goodbye* (1953), Chandler was discharged from the Royal Air Force on February 20, 1919 in Vancouver.

Raymond Chandler's final novel, *Playback* (1958), was set mostly in Esmerelda, California, featuring Philip Marlowe, but his earlier screenplay of the same name was mostly set in Vancouver. Published posthumously in New York by Mysterious Library, as *Raymond Chandler's Unknown Thriller* (1985), the revised screenplay/story opens with a beautiful blonde, Betty Mayfield, crossing the border on a train, having narrowly escaped being imprisoned for a murder she did not commit. In Vancouver she again becomes the prime suspect in a murder investigation. She writes a suicide note in the Hudson's Bay Department Store but she's dissuaded from killing herself by Brandon, a debonair millionaire who promises to help her by whisking her over to Victoria in his yacht. The Vancouver Police Department's Detective Killaine cleverly determines the murderer is Brandon, who is planning to kill Betty on his yacht. He rescues Betty with a helicopter.

Raymond Chandler was unusually well paid to write the script and took particular care to revise it. Although it contains excellent sardonic dialogue, and it carefully recognizes the cultural differences between Canada and the United States, Chandler had difficulty transcribing the screenplay into *Playback*, the novel. The screenplay lacks a cryptic first person narrator, something he corrected in the novel when he introduced his famous "hard-boiled" private detective, Philip Marlowe.

Raymond Chandler became president of the Mystery Writers of America and died of pneumonia brought on by an unusually heavy drinking binge on March 26, 1959.

W.O. Mitchell

Although he is mostly recognized as a prairie author, W.O. Mitchell spent many summers at his family's summer home at Mabel Lake, near Salmon Arm, BC, where he and his wife Myrna Mitchell shared good times with their children and grandchildren.

William Ormond Mitchell was born in Weyburn, Saskatchewan, in 1914 and died in Calgary in 1998. Most famously he wrote *Who Has Seen the Wind* (1947).

Leonard Cohen

And he showed us where to look "among the garbage and the flowers. . . ." The story goes that Dan McLeod and like-minded counter-culturalists decided to start a "peace paper" at a Vancouver party following a poetry reading by Leonard Cohen in February of 1967.

The first organizational meeting was held at the home of Rick Kitaeff on March 30, 1967. This subsequently gave rise to a cooperatively managed newspaper called the *Georgia Straight*, later controlled and owned by McLeod. The history is fuzzy, but certainly the newspaper had literary beginnings. Other poets involved in its creation included bill bissett — whose blewointmentpress printed a handbill advertising an open organizational meeting for April 2, 1967 — as well as Pierre Coupey, Gerry Gilbert and Milton Acorn.

Arthur Conan Doyle

During his fourth visit to North America in 1923 (following visits in 1894, 1914 and 1922), Sir Arthur Conan Doyle, the creator of the rationalist-hero detective Sherlock Holmes, travelled across Canada and the US to lecture on his favourite topic, Spiritualism. While travelling with his wife Lady Jean and their three children, Conan Doyle spoke in fifteen cities across the US, as well as Vancouver.

Conan Doyle's visit to Vancouver is mentioned in *Our Second American Adventure* (1924). He offers the following unusual analysis of the *Komagata Maru* incident of May, 1914:

"The whole incident seemed to me to be so grotesque — for why should sun-loving Hindus force themselves upon Canada — that I was convinced some larger purpose lay behind it. That purpose was, as we can now see, to promote discord among the races under the British flag. There can be no doubt that it was German money that chartered that ship."

How Kiplingesque.

Rabindranath Tagore

The first person from Asia to win the Nobel Prize for Literature, Bengali poet Sir Rabindranath Tagore (1861–1941) made four visits to North

America, and was photographed by Vancouver photographer John Vanderpant in 1929.

En route to California, Tagore was visiting BC as the keynote speaker for a conference of the National Council of Education, stopping only in Victoria and Vancouver. He spoke four times in Vancouver and once in Victoria. Aged nearly seventy at this time, Tagore had to cancel a proposed visit to the Victoria gurdwara for its Vaisakhi Day celebrations but was entertained by an evening of sacred music at the Vancouver gurdwara. Revered as a writer and as a spokesperson for Indian independence, Tagore was joined by his English translator and editor Charles Freer Andrews, a missionary who was also a close associate of Mahatma Gandhi.

"Do your very best to prove yourselves 'good Canadians,'" Tagore advised. As the bilingual guide for these two esteemed literary visitors, Kartar Singh of Toronto, a Theosophist, decided to remain in British Columbia where he befriended the thriving sawmill operator Kapoor Singh Siddoo and began to publish a bilingual English and Punjabi newspaper called *India and Canada: A Journal of Interpretation and Information*, producing seven monthly issues in 1929 and 1930.

Knighted in 1915, Tagore resigned the honour in 1919 to protest repressive British measures in India. Among his many books is *The Religion of Man*.

Theodore Roosevelt

While not widely recognized today as a literary man, Theodore Roosevelt, the twenty-sixth president of the United States, born in 1858, first rose to prominence as the twenty-three-year-old author of *The Naval War of 1812*, hailed as a literary and scholarly triumph. Roosevelt rose to military prominence due to jingoistic newspaper reports that inflated the heroism of his Rough Riders regiment as they overcame the outmanned, undersupplied Spanish opposition in Cuba in 1898.

When Roosevelt visited Vancouver in 1915, four years before he died, Mayor Louis Dennison Taylor outwitted his political foes by hopping on the train as it stopped in New Westminster, and then grabbing the spotlight upon Roosevelt's arrival in Vancouver by escorting him around Stanley Park in his car.

The man most famous for saying, "Speak softly, and carry a big stick; you will go far," received the Nobel Peace Prize in 1906.

Charles Bukowski

When notoriously foul-mouthed boozer Charles "Hank" Bukowski made his first trip to Canada in October of 1976, organizers for his Western Front reading were surprised that women in the audience far outnumbered men. That reading is described by Bukowski towards the end of his novel entitled *Women*. The reason for all the female attention, according to reading organizer Ted Laturnus, was that although Bukowski was slovenly and "genuinely physically ugly," he had "a soothing monotone voice and a full head of hair that reminded me of Fabian." At a post-reading party Bukowski didn't drink much and "was besieged with offers of congress." No matter where Bukowski went during his Vancouver visit, he "had to fight the women off," according to Jim Christy's *The BUK Book: Musings on Charles Bukowski* (ECW).

Charles Bukowski returned to give another Vancouver reading in 1979. After a night of dancing upon his arrival, he fell out of bed in the Sylvia Hotel and had to be taken to the hospital for stitches. The reading the following day at the Viking Inn was a raucous affair at which Bukowski was drunk and the audience heckled. There were approximately 650 people in the audience. It was the last Bukowski poetry reading that was recorded on film. Footage from that reading appears at the outset of *Bukowski: Born into This*, a 2003 documentary about Bukowski by John Dullaghan that was screened at Vancouver's Ridge Theatre in 2005.

During the making of the documentary, the filmmakers uncovered a videotaped record of the entire Bukowski performance that was made by Dennis B. Del Torre. This full-length performance by Bukowski has since been released as *There's Gonna Be a God Damn Riot in Here*.

Saul Bellow

Saul Bellow lived on Swan Lake on Vancouver Island in the spring of 1982 when he was a guest lecturer in the English department at the University of Victoria. There he reputedly wrote the title story for his book *Him with His Foot in His Mouth* (1984) about an American musicologist who has taken refuge in British Columbia.

Winston Churchill

Winston Churchill visited Vancouver with his son Randolph and his brother Jack in 1929. He opened the Annual Provincial Exhibition in New Westminster, commending a decision to proceed with the fair despite a fire on the grounds six weeks earlier. It was, he remarked, "the culmination of a courage that does not know defeat." He visited a logging company in Haney the next day. Afterwards he dined atop Grouse Mountain.

Although renowned as First Lord of the Admiralty, Secretary of State of War, Chancellor of the Exchequer and ultimately Prime Minister (1940–1945; 1951–1955), Churchill was also a gifted writer and rhetorician who wrote *The Second World War* and *A History of the English-Speaking Peoples*, along with other works. He began his career as a journalist covering the so-called Spanish-American War in Cuba.

Winston Churchill received the Nobel Prize for Literature in 1953.

Dylan Thomas

Dylan Thomas liked to say that he came to America to pursue "naked women in wet mackintoshes" but he was no Casanova. Short, sickly and alcoholic, he was nonetheless accorded rock star status in April of 1950, at age thirty-six, when he read poetry at the UBC auditorium before an audience of 1,300, after which he recited more English verse at the Hotel Vancouver's Mayfair Room.

At an after-party in his honour at a house on Davie Street, Dylan Thomas and Malcolm Lowry — who had already met one another in England — locked themselves into a room with some liquor. "By the time they came out," Earle Birney recalled, "neither of them was very comprehensible. Lowry was inclined to pass out early, and I guess I must have helped to get Dylan back to his hotel."

The Lowrys fell asleep in the house and woke up there the next morning, visited Dylan Thomas at the Hotel Vancouver, found him in bed with a female admirer (who Dylan Thomas promptly dismissed), and started drinking again.

In a letter to his wife, Caitlin Thomas, dated April 7, 1950, about this visit, Dylan Thomas wrote: "The city of Vancouver is a quite handsome hellhole. It is, of course, being Canadian, more British than Cheltenham. I spoke last night — or read, I never lecture, how could I? — in front of two huge Union Jacks.

"The pubs — they are called beer-parlours — serve only beer, are not allowed to have whiskey or wine or any spirits at all — and are open only for a few hours a day. There are, in this monstrous hotel, two bars, one for Men, one for Women. They do not mix.

"Today, Good Friday, nothing is open nor will be open all day long. Everybody is pious and patriotic, apart from a few people in the university & my old friend Malcolm Lowry — do you remember *Under the Volcano?* — who lives in a hut in the mountains & who came down to see me last night. . . .

"This afternoon I pick up my bag of soiled clothes and take a plane to Seattle. And thank God to be out of British Canada & back in the terrible United States of America."

During his second visit in 1952, Dylan Thomas insulted professors at the UBC Faculty Club and again got rip-roaring drunk. He died one year later in New York, at age thirty-nine, after a colossal whiskey binge. In 1996, Langara English instructor Ted Langley founded a Dylan Thomas Society in Vancouver.

Joseph Campbell

Joseph Campbell, the man who gave filmmaker George Lucas the archetypes for his *Star Wars* saga, visited the Queen Charlotte Islands in 1932. The visit came about because, during the Depression, Campbell was close friends with a self-taught California ecologist named Ed Ricketts and a would-be novelist named John Steinbeck. Ricketts made three excursions to British Columbia in 1932 (with Campbell), 1945 and 1946 to collect marine specimens. Steinbeck later modelled several characters in his fiction on Ricketts, including "Doc" in the 1945 novel *Cannery Row*.

Ed Ricketts died when he was hit by a train near Cannery Row in May of 1948. At the time he and Steinbeck had been planning a trip to British Columbia to satisfy Rickett's intention to write a book about BC coastal marine life to be called *Beyond the Outer Shores*.

In 2004, at age thirty-two, Ucluelet-raised journalist Eric Enno Tamm published the first biography of Ed Ricketts called *Beyond the Outer Shores* (Raincoast 2004). Whereas the sometimes stormy relationship between Ricketts and Steinbeck was well known, *Beyond the Outer Shores* provided fresh insights into the friendship between the two men.

Tamm's history of the friendship and rivalries between Steinbeck, Campbell and Ricketts contains a section outlining the three-month voyage made by Campbell and Ricketts around the Queen Charlotte Islands in 1932 in the *Grampus*, a small cruising vessel. At the time, the yet-to-be-esteemed philosopher Joseph Campbell was escaping the wrath of Steinbeck for cultivating an affair with Steinbeck's wife Carol.

William Burroughs

William Burroughs first gained notoriety as a result of a censorship battle regarding his 1953 paperback, *Junkie*. Associated with the Beat poets of San Francisco and City Lights Books, he is renowned for his 1959 memoir of heroin addiction entitled *Naked Lunch*. Burroughs screened his films and read from his works at 111 Dunsmuir Street on November 17, 1974, and returned in 1988, staying at the Sylvia Hotel, for a Western Front exhibit of his "shotgun art" — paint gun splats onto plywood that he sold by mail until his death on August 2, 1997.

Burroughs' presence influenced the evolution of experimental writing in Vancouver, and in 1999, events were held at the grunt gallery in Vancouver dedicated to Burroughs.

Rudyard Kipling

The most enthusiastic reception given to a visiting writer in British Columbia was accorded to Rudyard Kipling — the chief literary cheerleader for the British Empire — when he addressed the one-year-old Canadian Club at the Pender Hall in 1907. It was the same year he received the Nobel Prize for Literature.

When Rudyard Kipling first arrived in Vancouver, during his "wedding tour" of 1892, the City Solicitor, George Hamersley, a member of the Inner Bar, London, was asked if he might greet the visiting writer. "Kipling! Who the devil is Kipling?" the lawyer reportedly said. "Never heard of the man!"

Kipling greatly admired the efficiency of the Royal Canadian Mounted Police. "Always the marvel to which Canadians seem insensible," he wrote, "was that on one side of an imaginary line should be Safety, Law, Honour and Obedience, and on the other, frank, brutal decivilization."

Kipling was so pleased with Vancouver that he purchased a town lot in the Mount Pleasant area prior to embarking for Japan from the CPR dock on the Empress of India on April 4, 1892. "He that sold it to me was a delightful English boy," Kipling later wrote in *American Notes*. "All the boy said was, 'I give you my word it isn't on a cliff or under water, and before long the town ought to move out that way.' And I took it as easily as a man buys a piece of tobacco.

"I became owner of 400 well-developed pines, thousands of tons of granite scattered in blocks at the roots of the pines, and a sprinkling of earth. That's a town lot in Vancouver.

"You or your agent hold onto it till property rises, then sell out and buy more land farther out of town and repeat the process. I do not quite see how this sort of thing helps the growth of a town, but the English boy says it is the 'essence of speculation' so it must be all right. But I wish there were fewer pines and rather less granite on the ground."

Kipling was duped. When he returned in 1907, he learned that he'd been paying taxes on property legally owned by someone else. Privately, Kipling wrote, "All the consolation we got from the smiling people of Vancouver was: "You bought that from Steve, did you? Ah-hah, Steve! You hadn't ought to ha' bought from Steve. No! Not from Steve!' And thus did the good Steve cure us of speculating in real estate."

In 1907, Kipling was met by the mayor, the Board of Trade and provincial government members. An audience of 500 attended his luncheon speech. Women weren't invited; there was not enough room. But women came anyway, crowding the hall to its doors, filling the spectator gallery.

After receiving a standing, cheering ovation and a Moroccan leather case, embossed with his initials, containing his honorary lifetime membership to the Canadian Club, Kipling rose to discourse on Vancouver. He compared the city to the head of an army bravely passing through the mountains "to secure a stable Western civilization facing the Eastern Sea." Frequently interrupted by applause, he added, "If I had not as great faith as I have in our breed, and in our race, I would tremble at your responsibilities."

Kipling was a vitriolic racist, constantly spewing venom about Huns, Yids and Micks. He was equally contemptuous of trade unionists, liberals and suffragettes. He ominously advised, "The time is coming when you will have to choose between the desired reinforcements of your own stock and blood, and the undesired races to whom you are strangers, whose speech you do not understand, and from whose instincts and traditions you are separated by thousands of years." When asked by a reporter for the *Vancouver World* about "the all-absorbing topic of Hindoo immigration," Kipling confided he "had come six thousand miles to study it."

Kipling was wildly enthusiastic about Victoria, having first visited the city in 1889. He wrote, "Real estate agents recommend it as a little piece of England — the island on which it stands is about the size of Great Britain — but no England is set in any such seas or so fully charged with the mystery of the larger ocean beyond. . . . I tried honestly to render something of the colour, the gaiety, and the graciousness of the town and the island, but only found myself piling up unbelievable adjectives, and so let it go with a hundred other wonders."

Nary a word was printed about his property loss in Vancouver.

Dalai Lama

The 14th Dalai Lama, Tenzin Gyatso, visited Seattle in 1979 and held a special audience for the representatives of the Tibetan Refugee Aid Society (TRAS), the Vancouver-based organization started by his friends George and Ingeborg Woodcock after they met him in Dharamsala, India, in 1961.

The Dalai Lama's first visit to Vancouver the following year was organized by T.C. Tethong of Victoria, the Dalai Lama's translator following his escape from Tibet in 1959 with the help of the CIA.

Having received the Nobel Prize for Peace in 1989, the Dalai Lama made his second visit to Vancouver in July of 1993, at which time he had a private meeting with the Woodcocks.

He returned in April of 2004 and September of 2006. A fifth visit is scheduled for September of 2009, chiefly organized by Victor Chan of Bowen Island, author of an extensive traveller's guide to Tibet.

For his fourth Vancouver visit in September of 2006, he planned to visit Ingeborg Woodcock, widow of George Woodcock, but she had died several months earlier.

A monk who rises for prayer on a daily basis between four and five a.m., the Dalai Lama is also credited as being the author of numerous bestselling titles, some of which were written with the assistance of a ghost writer. The major autobiographical works are *My Land and My People* (1962), *Freedom in Exile* (1991) and *Ethics for the New Millennium* (2001).

Pope John Paul

By far the most travelled pope in history, Pope John Paul II became the first non-Italian pope since Hadrian VI (1522–1523) in 1978. He visited nearly every country willing to receive him, including Canada in 1984.

Born as Karol Wojtyla in Wadowice, Poland, he wrote numerous books, including an autobiography, *Gift and Mystery: On the Fiftieth Anniversary of My Priestly Ordination*. A book about his visit was produced for the archdiocese of Vancouver.

Arthur Hailey

The former Vancouver International Airport, now used for small planes, was the model for the airport that appears in the climax of Arthur Hailey's *Flight into Danger*, a 1956 television movie in which half of a plane's passengers and its crew are afflicted by food poisoning due to fish dinners. Hailey, a former pilot in WWII, imagined this scenario while taking a flight from Toronto to Vancouver, and experiencing Canadian airline food.

The almost brand-new TV network called the Canadian Broadcasting Corporation or the CBC (only four years old) bought Hailey's script for $600. The pivotal role of the emergency pilot was played by a young James Doohan, who later became widely known as "Scottie" on *Star Trek*. The airing was an unprecedented success for the fledgling CBC, leading to a screening in Britain.

Hailey's script became the basis for a 1957 Paramount movie called *Zero Hour*. A novelized version of this story, co-authored by John Castle, was released in 1958. One year later it was published in the United States as *Runway Zero-Eight*, marking the start of Arthur Hailey's fiction career.

Hailey's thriller *Airport* was researched in Los Angeles and Chicago; his blockbuster novel *Hotel* was based on the Fairmont New Orleans Hotel. But his writing career — one can argue — took off from Vancouver.

Thor Heyerdahl

Before he became famous for sailing the *Kon-Tiki* from Peru to the atoll Raroia in the South Pacific, Norwegian explorer and archaeologist Thor Heyerdahl visited Bella Coola for about two years (1939–1940) to compare petroglyphs at Thorsen Creek with Polynesian art forms. He had theorized that Hawaii could have been settled by people from British Columbia.

During his visit, when Germany overran Norway, Heyerdahl was forced to remain in Canada with limited funds. Befriending guide and hunter Clayton Mack, he received help from Mack to visit pictographs at Kwatna Inlet, whereupon Heyerdahl asked his resourceful Nuxalk guide if he thought it would be possible for his ancestors to have reached Hawaii in a dugout canoe. Clayton Mack suggested they might have used giant rafts of kelp.

Lady Dufferin

In 1876 Lady Dufferin visited British Columbia with Lord Dufferin, Governor General of Canada. Her impressions of Canada are contained in *My Canadian Journal 1872–8: Extracts from My Letters Home Written While Lord Dufferin Was Governor-General* (A. Appleton, 1891). Some of Lady Dufferin's watercolours of BC are housed at Library and Archives Canada in Ottawa.

As one of the great role models for women in the late 1800s, Lady Dufferin epitomized progressive civility.

Brother XII

British Columbia's most fantastic cult leader, known to his followers as Brother XII, Edward Arthur Wilson was a theosophical leader who had a spiritual community on southern Vancouver Island in the late 1920s and early 1930s.

The financial and sexual scandals that arose from his Aquarian

Foundation settlement have led to comparisons with various eccentrics such as Rasputin, scientologist L. Ron Hubbard and Jonestown fanatic Jim Jones. Wilson has been more fairly dubbed Canada's False Messiah or False Prophet.

Infamous for his egotism and fraudulent behaviour, Wilson is rarely cited as a literary figure. Yet he spread his delusionary claptrap in various publications and books: *The Three Truths* (1927); *The Aquarian Foundation* (1927); *Foundation Letters and Teachings* (1927); *The End of the Days* (1928); *Unsigned Letters from an Elder Brother* (1930); and *Primer of Astrology for Children* (1930).

Books about him include *Canada's False Prophet* (1967) by Herbert Emerson Wilson and *The Devil of Decourcey Island* (1989) by Charles Lillard, Ron MacIsaac and Don Clark. The main biography is *Brother Twelve: The Incredible Story of Canada's False Prophet and His Doomed Cult of Gold, Sex, and Black Magic* (1992) by John Oliphant.

Mark Twain

One of the first literary luminaries to appear in British Columbia was the American humorist Mark Twain, alias for Samuel Clemens, who spoke to a delighted throng at the Imperial Theatre on August 15, 1895. He received rave reviews but came down with a bad cold, which left him recuperating at the Hotel Vancouver.

Kurt Vonnegut & Mark Vonnegut

The son of novelist Kurt Vonnegut, Mark Vonnegut grew up in Cape Cod and studied religion at (Quaker) Swarthmore College in Pennsylvania. Upon his graduation in 1969, at age twenty-one, in order to evade the draft and escape the shadow of his father, he drove to British Columbia in a Volkswagen van with his girlfriend Virginia and their dog Zeke. He briefly worked at Duthie Books.

In an effort to adopt the hippie lifestyle, Mark Vonnegut retreated to a coastal commune at Powell Lake, located 18 kilometres by boat from the nearest road or electricity, where his experimentation with drugs led to a severe descent into anguish, during which time he imagined he was responsible for a California earthquake that had killed his girlfriend. He was nonetheless accorded the status of mystic on the commune, which included some of his friends from Swarthmore College.

Emaciated, suicidal and delusional, Mark Vonnegut developed bizarre notions, such as a belief that he had communicated with every great artist in history. Aliens were out to get him. . . . On Valentine's Day 1971, following intervention by his father, he was committed to Hollywood Psychiatric Hospital in New Westminster where he was diagnosed as being severely schizophrenic. "My son Mark's most unsociable performance when [he was] bananas, and before I could get him into a Canadian laughing academy," Kurt Vonnegut later wrote, "was to babble on and on, and then wing a cue ball through a picture window in an urban commune in Vancouver, British Columbia. It was only then that his flower children friends telephoned me to say he was in need of a father. God bless telephones.

"Mark's dear mother, Jane Marie, née Cox, now dead, a Quaker and, like Mark, a graduate of Swarthmore, would often tell him that he was supposed to save the world. His college major had been religion, and he had not yet considered becoming what he has indeed become, a pediatrician. One seeming possibility before he went nuts was that he study for the Unitarian ministry.

"He was then twenty-two, and I myself was a mere spring chicken of forty-seven, a mere thirty-two years ago. By the time Mark and I went in a hired car from the house with the broken picture window in Vancouver to what turned out to be an excellent private mental hospital in nearby New Westminster, he had at least become a jazz saxophonist and a painter. He babbled merrily en route and it was language, but the words were woven into vocal riffs worthy of his hero John Coltrane."

The Eden Express: A Memoir of Insanity (Praeger/Bantam, 1975) by Mark Vonnegut describes his difficulties with drugs and schizophrenia between 1969 and 1972. It was written after Vonnegut accepted his need for medication and returned to the society from whence he came. Initially Mark Vonnegut wrote an article entitled "Why I Want to Bite R. D. Laing."

Having first attributed his recovery to orthomolecular (megavitamin) therapy, he later came to the conclusion that he had been manic-depressive for hereditary reasons. Mark Vonnegut subsequently studied medicine at Harvard Medical School and became a pediatrician in Boston.

Tennessee Williams

One of the most important playwrights of the 20th century, Tennessee Williams, attempted to rekindle his flagging career by accepting an invitation to workshop his revised play *The Red Devil Battery Sign* at the Vancouver Playhouse. This play was supposed to have received its world premiere in BC in 1980, directed by Roger Hodgman. In fact, *The Red Devil Battery Sign* had already flopped once before when it was first produced in Boston in 1975.

Reviews were, at best, mixed. Nonetheless, the city was sufficiently flattered by Williams' gushy praise for its hospitality (in public, at least) that America's most influential playwright was invited to return as a Distinguished Writer in Residence at the University of British Columbia in 1981.

Upon his return, the UBC Theatre Department mounted his rewritten version of Anton Chekhov's *The Seagull*, staged as *The Notebook of Trigorin*. The department was also happy to be the first to publish the revised script for *The Red Devil Battery Sign* in UBC's literary periodical *Prism international*.

Born Thomas Lanier Williams in 1911 in Missouri, he changed his first name to Tennessee in 1939. Starting with *The Glass Menagerie* in 1944, he achieved a remarkable string of successful plays into the 1950s, winning the Pulitzer Prize for *A Streetcar Named Desire* and *Cat on a Hot Tin Roof*.

A drug addict, he choked to death on a pill bottle cap in 1983.

Yevgeny Yevtushenko

The Russian poet Yevgeny Yevtushenko was celebrated outside of Russia in the 1960s and 1970s as an emerging new, liberal voice within the Soviet Union. He visited Vancouver in 1974 and gave a packed reading at the Vancouver Art Gallery. Pulp Press publisher Steve Osborne has described the subsequent dinner with Yevtushenko and Vancouver literati at Orestes restaurant in his collection of essays *Ice & Fire: Dispatches from the New World, 1988–1998* (Arsenal Pulp).

Miscellaneous References

When *Vancouver Sun* journalist Mark Hume accepted the Roderick Haig-Brown Prize in 1999 for *River of the Angry Moon, Seasons on the Bella Coola* (Greystone), co-written with Harvey Thommasen, he said, "I don't really know how to thank someone who's dead, but I do feel I should mention his name tonight: Ted Hughes, a poet-laureate of Great Britain. He used to slip into British Columbia every few years and fish the rivers for steelhead. He gave me a great deal of encouragement for this book. He was inspirational to me shortly before he died. He knew that the rivers of British Columbia are not to be taken lightly."

The author of *Lady Chatterley's Lover* once wrote in a letter from Sicily on October 9, 1921: "My plan is, ultimately, to get a little farm somewhere by myself, in Mexico, New Mexico, Rocky Mountains, or British Columbia." The comment was made in a letter to Earl Brewster, reproduced in *The Letters of D.H. Lawrence, IV* (Cambridge University Press, 1987), edited by W. Roberts, J.T. Boulton and E. Mansfield.

In the novel *The Small House at Allington*, published by *The Cornhill Magazine* between 1862 and 1864, Anthony Trollope's protagonist John Eames is so forlorn and disheartened by love that he considers fleeing to the ends of the earth, asking, "Had he not better go to Australia or Vancouver Island, or ____?"

The first literary reference to the area now called British Columbia occurs in the second book of *Gulliver's Travels*, a fictional work by satirist Jonathan Swift. Caught in a storm "so that the oldest sailor on board could not tell in what part of the World we were," narrator Lemuel Gulliver sails up the northwest coast of America in 1703 to a land of giants called Brobdingnag. Swift also included a map showing Brobdingnag was north of New Albion, a term used by Sir Francis Drake to describe the west coast after his secret voyage of 1579. Hence Brobdingnag approximates present-day BC.

[2009]

Malcolm Lowry Forever

―⌒ A.T.

■ Malcolm Lowry — the eternally constipated, accident-prone, self-exiled, alcoholic syphilophobe who lived in BC for fourteen years at his father's expense — refuses to die. Anarchists, musicians and academics recently staged a Malcolm Lowry Festival at Cates Park, near where Malcolm and Margerie Lowry lived in their famous squatter's shack, and Michael Turner organized a reading series at the Malcolm Lowry Room in a Burnaby beer parlour. Academics have long been fascinated by the Lowry story and regularly make the trek to UBC Library's Special Collections, which hosts the world's foremost archive of materials pertaining to the author of *Under the Volcano* — due largely to the efforts of librarians Ann Yandle and Basil Stuart-Stubbs. Gordon Bowker's *Pursued by Furies: A Life of Malcolm Lowry* (Random House, 1993), which comes in at 672 pages, is justified on the grounds that it is the first comprehensive biography since the 1988 death of Lowry's second wife, a fellow alcoholic who jealously guarded the Lowry mythology and prevented research.

LOWRYPHILES CAN NOW learn from Gordon Bowker's exhaustive biography that Lowry dealt with his problem of premature ejaculation by singing "The Star-Spangled Banner" and that he abandoned his notion of becoming a Canadian citizen when Social Credit was elected. "Mc-Carthy is their hero," he claimed. After the film *The Wild One* was banned in BC, Lowry referred to W.A.C. Bennett's gang as Strong-armed Stink-weasels.

Bowker reveals much about Lowry's childhood and his brutally cold father, taking as his cue a statement by Edmund Leach that "the family, with its narrow privacy and tawdry secrets, is the course of all our discontents." In his youth Lowry feared going blind from masturbation. His extreme fear of contracting syphilis, which is already well known, did not prevent him from having sex with prostitutes as a schoolboy. He claimed drinking was a sexual substitute, begun in his teens to compensate for a lack of sexual skill. As well, Lowry feared authority, especially the police, and worried about being spied on. He also worried about being rejected by women and, curiously enough, being exposed as a plagiarist.

"Perhaps he never grew up," says Bowker, "and the remarkable thing is that the small boy, so relentlessly pursued by the avenging agents of fate, survived to the age of almost forty-eight." Appallingly self-conscious, Lowry was tormented by the "tyranny of self" throughout his life. Although he didn't wish to be cured of alcoholism, he underwent electric shock treatments, Methedrine sessions and aversion therapy while under psychiatric observation in the 1950s.

Pursued by Furies airs all the unsavoury details, including Margerie Lowry's role in Lowry's very mysterious death "by misadventure," as outlined in the section called "Going Down Fighting." After having left Canada, Lowry pined for his Dollarton shack and was beginning to realize that he could manage life without Margerie, but she on her part absolutely refused to return to primitive life in Canada. She also knew that if they ever divorced she would lose any inheritance, including control of the manuscripts which she had a large part in co-producing.

Mindreader

Lowry and Margerie fought: he reputedly attacked her with a broken gin bottle; she reputedly fled to a neighbour's. His body was discovered the next morning. A bottle of 20 sodium amytal sleeping tablets belonging to Margerie was missing, then later found empty in her drawer. Medical evidence indicated acute barbiturate poisoning and alcoholism. In fact he died by inhaling his own vomit.

The doctor refused to sign the death certificate and police were called. "From the beginning, Lowry's friends were uncomfortable not only about the apparent circumstances of the death but also about the garbled and contradictory versions of events which Margerie had begun to recount," says Bowker.

Margerie was admitted to Hellingly Mental Hospital the day after the funeral. After friends thoroughly searched Malcolm's belongings and found nothing, Margerie claimed to have found a suicide note from him ten days later, which she said she destroyed. Malcolm's doctor did not believe her, partly because Lowry had so often said he believed suicide was an offence against the spirit. "Her line was that he had committed suicide but she had managed to persuade a sympathetic coroner to hand down a verdict of 'Misadventure' to save his reputation and her suffering at the hands of the press," says Bowker.

Margerie had frequently fed Lowry handfuls of vitamin pills during his countless drunken bouts, saying this helped him cope with a hangover the next day. Bowker tactfully suggests that Lowry could have swallowed what he thought were vitamin pills on the night of June 26, 1957 — or, if the pills weren't accidentally self-administered; they could have been administered by someone else.

After testifying at the inquest that she had stayed at a neighbour's, Margerie later lied about leaving Lowry alone for the night. "Suicide was Margerie's version, which no one believed," Bowker concludes, "and she did hint that she had not told all, even to Lowry's closest friends, but she was to take that dark secret with her to her grave."

[1993]

Appreciating Alice

—ᴼ A.T.

■ Alice Munro, arguably the finest writer this country has produced, received the George Woodcock Lifetime Achievement Awards in Vancouver in 2005. She was awarded the Man Booker International Prize in 2009 in recognition of a body of work that has contributed to fiction on the world stage. That same year Munro was honoured with a tribute at the 22nd Vancouver International Writers and Readers Festival, leading to this appreciation.

MOST ARTISTS END UP imitating themselves. Their art degenerates into a copy of a copy of a copy. Alice Munro has remained a great artist for five decades because her stories are propelled by curiosity. Human nature (not moralism) is always the catalyst, and human nature has endless variations. Life in Alice Munro's fiction is frequently painful and disappointing — but the reflex of humour can be a crucial antidote.

Now seventy-eight, Alice Munro raised her three daughters mostly in West Vancouver and Victoria, where her first husband Jim Munro, father of her children, still owns and operates Munro's Books (est. 1963). She remains more of a West Coaster than most of her readers realize. "I like the West Coast attitudes," she told CBC Radio in 2004. "Winters [in BC] to me are sort of like a holiday. People are thinking about themselves. The way I grew up [in Ontario], people were thinking about duty."

She has always been a writer. During her acceptance of the Man Booker International Prize at Trinity College in Dublin, Munro recalled being seven years old, pacing in her backyard, trying to find a way to make Hans Christian Andersen's *The Little Mermaid* have a happy ending. Her new collection of stories is called *Too Much Happiness* (Douglas Gibson Books, M&S). Simultaneously, there is a new edition of *My Best Stories* (Penguin), with an introduction by Margaret Atwood.

Alice Munro was born Alice Laidlaw in Wingham, Ontario, on July 10, 1931. Her father was a farmer; her mother, a former teacher. When her mother developed Parkinson's disease, the young Alice handled the brunt of domestic duties while all the while nursing ambitions to become a writer. "I think choosing to be a writer was a very reckless thing to do," she told CBC's Shelagh Rogers in 2004, "although I didn't realize it. I was planning an historical novel in grade seven. It gave way to a *Wuthering Heights* novel I was writing all the way through high school."

During her two years at the University of Western Ontario, she published her first short story in *Folio*, an undergraduate literary magazine, and met fellow student Jim Munro. They married in December of 1951 and moved to Vancouver where their two eldest daughters were born. Another daughter died of kidney failure on the day she was born.

In Vancouver, Alice Munro befriended Margaret Laurence, another housewife who was learning to write, and she was inspired by the success of local novelist Ethel Wilson. In Victoria, where a fourth daughter was born in 1966, she helped operate Munro's Books, considered one of the finest independent bookstores in Canada. In all, Alice Munro resided in Vancouver and Victoria for twenty-two years before her first marriage ended and she moved back to Ontario.

After separating from her husband in 1973, Munro became writer-in-residence at the University of Western Ontario in 1974. In 1975, she moved to Clinton, Ontario, in Huron County, with a former university friend, Gerald Fremlin, a geographer, partially in order to help look after his mother. Clinton is located approximately 35 kilometres from Wingham where she grew up. (The issue of *Folio* in which she had first published a short story also contained a story by Fremlin, who is slightly older than she is.)

Alice Munro married Fremlin after she was divorced in 1976, the year she received her first honorary doctorate (having been unable to finish university due to lack of funds). They now divide their time between residences in Clinton in Ontario and Comox on Vancouver Island.

Encouraged by CBC Radio's Robert Weaver since 1951, Alice Munro sold her first short story to *Mayfair* magazine in 1953. She has suggested she might have opted for the short story approach to fiction because she was balancing her duties as the mother of three children, but she also spent many of her formative years as writer trying to write a novel without success.

Alice Munro's first short story collection, *Dance of the Happy Shades* (1968), received the Governor General's Award for Fiction. *Lives of Girls and Women* (1971), which was marketed as a novel and received the Canadian Booksellers Award, was the basis for a Canadian movie of the same name; it featured her daughter Jenny Munro as the heroine Del Jordan. Recently Sarah Polley's superb cinematic adaptation of Alice Munro's story *The Bear Came Over the Mountain*, renamed *Away from Her* and starring Julie Christie and Gordon Pinsent, was nominated for an Academy Award for Best Adapted Screenplay.

A frequent contributor to the *New Yorker* since 1976, Alice Munro became the eleventh recipient of the George Woodcock Lifetime Achievement Award for BC writing in 2005. She accepted the award, accompanied by her daughter, *BCBW* contributor Sheila Munro, at the Vancouver Public Library, where she once worked.

Alice Munro is only the third recipient of the new Man Booker International Prize. Part of her appeal is that her work is distinctly Canadian in a classic "Who Do You Think You Are?" mold. Typically, she told her Man Booker audience in Ireland that writing, for her, has amounted to ". . . always fooling around with what you find. . . . This is what you want to do with your time — and people give you a prize for it."

In "Fiction," one of several brilliant stories in *Too Much Happiness*, a graduate of the UBC Creative Writing program has published her first collection of stories called *How Are We to Live*. The protagonist, Joyce, is an older woman who once gave this girl music lessons as a child. She has realized this up-'n'-coming writer is the daughter of the woman to whom she lost her first husband when they were all living at a place called Rough River, decades before. Curiosity sends Joyce to the author's book launch at a North Vancouver bookstore. Classically Canadian, Munro writes, "Joyce has never understood this business of lining up to get a glimpse of the author and then going away with a stranger's name written in your book."

The self-confident young author (possibly a parody of Munro as a young writer?) has written a story that completely documents the domestic complications she witnessed, the intrigues that led to Joyce's divorce, and yet she does not recognize her former music teacher in the flesh. There is a poster of the self-centred first-time author wearing a little black jacket, tailored, severe, very low in the neck and, Munro adds, "Though she has practically nothing there to show off."

The inexperienced writer has simply reiterated reality without going to the trouble of fictionalizing it, adding nuances of her own. This writer ". . . sits there and writes her name as if that is all the writing she could be responsible for in this world." This is as scathing as Alice Munro gets. Then there is a reprieve for the reader, a line break. The once-jilted Joyce, who has since remarried to a sixty-five-year-old neuropsychologist, leaves the book launch. Alice Munro adds her final paragraph. "Walking up Lonsdale Avenue, walking uphill, she gradually regains her composure. This might even turn into a funny story that she would tell some day. She wouldn't be surprised." Munro doesn't write whodunnits in the Agatha Christie-style, but she does reveal the mysteries of behaviour. Conventional thinking is never enough.

[2009]

Alice Munro's *Too Much Happiness*

⟿ W.P. KINSELLA

■ In her 2009 collection of short stories, *Too Much Happiness*, Alice Munro explores a variety of intriguing, fresh, and introspective themes. She considers the challenges of the digital age, investigates the differences between fact and fiction, and leads the reader down darkened paths that evoke Flannery O'Connor. With striking language and wonderful humour, this collection is vintage Munro. Here W.P. Kinsella discusses *Too Much Happiness* and shares his admiration of Munro's ability to write into her seventies while remaining one of "the world's finest living short fiction writers."

I'LL NEVER FORGET what Alice Munro said to me the first time we met. She had come to Calgary to read. I purchased her book. I believe it was *The Moons of Jupiter*, and thoroughly enjoyed it, but it had not occurred to me that most of the stories contained a lot of humour. The audience laughed heartily at the story Alice read, one I had read in all seriousness. I said to her after the reading, "It never occurred to me that your story was funny."

Her reply was, "Bill, everything is funny."

Her new collection, *Too Much Happiness* (Douglas Gibson Books / M&S), contains ten delectable stories that are as good as anything she has written in her long career. The collection is vintage Munro in that many of the stories are novels, covering years and lifetimes, condensed to their tasty essence. The language as always is crisp and clear, like the tinkling of bells. Reading becomes a compulsion: one has to find out what is going to happen.

In "Deep-Holes," the character Sally has to deal with a son, who at age nine falls into a deep hole and is rescued by his father. The boy becomes a strange, troubled, possibly insane adult, who disappears for years at a time. Here Munro comments on the difficulty of possessing specialized knowledge and how this era of the internet diminishes that knowledge. When her son was young they scoured books for information on obscure and isolated islands like Tristan da Cunha. Years later, wanting to brush up on those details, she thinks of the encyclopedia, but ends up on the internet where every imaginable fact about Tristan da Cunha is displayed. She no longer has secret knowledge, and feels a terrible disappointment.

In the opening story "Dimensions," Doree's husband is in an institution for the criminally insane, having committed an unspeakable crime. Still, Doree visits him, unable to break the control he wielded over her. She listens to his manipulative ramblings and is tempted to accept his babble of other dimensions. She returns to reality literally with a crash, when she happens on an accident scene, and takes control of her own life by saving the life of a young accident victim. The language is striking: "A trickle of pink foam came out from under the boy's head, near the ear. It did not look like blood at all, but like the stuff you skim off from strawberries when you're making jam."

The story "Fiction," my favourite in this exemplary collection, deals with the question of what is fact and what is fiction, and does a writer really know where a story comes from? Or, for that matter, what a story is really about. I'm reminded of Henry James protesting that *The Turn of the Screw* was merely an entertainment, negating the volumes of psycho-babble written about the novel.

"Fiction" contains some wonderful humour that I didn't miss. Here is

Alice Munro describing a self-centred young author's first book: "*How Are We to Live* is the book's title. A collection of short stories, not a novel. This in itself is a disappointment. It seems to diminish the book's authority, making the author seem like somebody who is just hanging on to the gates of Literature, rather than safely settled inside."

"Free Radicals," the title a strong play on words, is about a home invasion. The invader, young, dangerous and slightly insane, enters the home of a widow living in a semi-rural area. The story sent me running to re-read Flannery O'Connor's "A Good Man is Hard to Find," the tale of an escaped convict and his pals executing a family in the rural South. In O'Connor's story the sense of menace is palpable, in Munro's it is muted. "Free Radicals" is more about the widow, Nita, learning about herself and what she is capable of, as she concocts a story, trying to win the invader's trust, about committing a murder herself. Only the *deus ex machina* ending is a little too pat, about the only soft spot in the whole collection.

The criminal shows Nita a photo of his family whom he murdered earlier in the day. ". . . it was the younger woman who monopolized the picture. Distinct and monstrous in her bright muumuu, dark hair done

up in a row of little curls along her forehead, cheeks sloping into her neck. And in spite of all that bulge of flesh an expression of some satisfaction and cunning."

"Child's Play," the story of two very young girls at summer camp, explores the banality of evil, and how disturbing events put behind us will just never stay in their place.

"Too Much Happiness," the title story, is vastly different from the other nine, but no less accomplished. It describes the final journey of a real life person, Russian mathematical genius Sophia Kovalevsky, a woman who was far ahead of her time, and who was an inspiration to women of her time, and is still a model to aspiring scientists. Her genius was not fully acknowledged. ". . . they kissed her hand and presented her with speeches and flowers. . . . But they had closed their doors when it came to giving her a job. They would no more think of that than of employing a learned chimpanzee." The Swedish were less discriminatory and she found employment in Stockholm. "The wives of Stockholm invited her into their houses. . . . They praised her and showed her off. . . . She might have been an oddity there, but she was an oddity that they approved of."

One of the reasons I retired from fiction writing in my sixties, besides feeling that I had said most of what I wanted to say, was that I have seen so many elderly writers trading on their name and turning out pitiful parodies of their former greatness: Updike and Mailer immediately come to mind. Therefore, it was a relief to find that Munro has not lost a step, and that the quality of this collection matches anything she has written in her long career.

In my forty-some years on the CanLit scene, an industry rife with jealousies, feuds and petty backbiting, to which I have contributed my share, I have never heard anyone say anything unkind about Alice Munro, personally or professionally. When Alice wins a prize, other writers and critics are not lined up to name ten books that should have won. Now Alice Munro has won the prestigious Man Booker International Prize. In my opinion she and Irish writer William Trevor are the world's finest living short fiction writers, something the Nobel Prize people might well consider.

[2009]

"British Columbia Has Always Been the Right Place for Me"

—ᴕ W.P. KINSELLA

■ W.P. Kinsella received the George Woodcock Lifetime Achievement Award in 2009. In terms of international readership, he has few peers in British Columbia. Here he reflects upon his writing career.

PUBLISHING IS MUCH like the movies; no one has a clue as to what will be successful, and when something is successful it is immediately imitated by twenty copycats.

I have had great good fortune in my writing career by, time after time, being in the right place at the right time. I am really happy that I am not starting out as a writer in today's climate, for I don't see any way I could break into the market and make a good living as I have done for the past 30-some years. While my novels have been successful, I favour the short story because I feel it is a much more complex and interesting form of expression.

My first experience of being in the right place at the right time was enrolling in some creative writing courses at the University of Victoria in 1970. I was raising a young family, managing my own business, and writing madly in all direction. My first creative writing instructor, Derk Wynand, had a huge folder for the twenty-page stories I was churning out each week, and one small folder for the remaining fifteen-plus students.

The very under-appreciated poet Robin Skelton was the first to recognize that buried deep in my meandering stories there might be seeds of talent. He told me about the great poet Stephen Spender who would write a hundred lines a day and be delighted if two of them eventually became usable. I got the message.

Then W.D. Valgardson came to teach at UVic. His story collection *Bloodflowers* influenced me greatly. From it I learned about great opening lines. Valgardson would take one of my twenty-page run-on sentences and tear off the first page, then scissor off half of the second page. He would then tear off the final two or three pages and say, "You warmed up for a page and a half before you started your story, you wound down for three pages after you finished it. Don't do that."

I'm a quick learner. Suddenly, in 1974, I had five stories accepted by literary magazines in a single week, and I've published virtually everything I've written since then. If it hadn't been for Bill Valgardson I might still be driving a cab in Victoria, with several suitcases of unpublished manuscripts under my bed.

It wasn't just having my talent recognized, it was the fact that short stories, which were considered a second-class art form in Canada, suddenly came into vogue. My slyly funny and subversive Silas Ermineskin stories were considered daring and groundbreaking and became in great demand by virtually every literary magazine in the country. Some editors expected me to lavish praise on them for daring to publish my stories. My first collection, *Dance Me Outside* in 1976, published by Michael Macklem at Oberon Press, had no advance, no publicity, but it became a best seller with a few good reviews and a whole lot of word-of-mouth, and still sells well thirty-three years later. I know people who bought twenty-five copies and sent them to their friends. A young assistant at Longhouse Books in Toronto, Jan Whitehouse, made me a personal project and touted my book to everyone who came into the store. All through the '80s and '90s my multiple story collections sold very well. Was it the chicken or the egg? Did my stories make the short story form acceptable again, or was I just in the right place at the right time?

British Columbia has always been the right place for me. I've been here since 1967, except for two years at graduate school in Iowa, and five horrible years, each one longer than the one before, at Desolate U. in Calgary, where anything creative was regarded with suspicion if not downright hostility, and where my time was wasted teaching bonehead English to students so unprepared for university that 90 percent of them should never have been allowed on a campus unless they were bussing tables in the cafeteria.

I was also in the right place at the right time when my novel *Shoeless Joe* was published in 1982. With that publication I discovered that there was a market for baseball fiction. Precious little had been done in the genre: there was little more than Malamud's depressing *The Natural* and the difficult-to-read *Great American Novel* by Philip Roth. There was no one taking advantage of the baseball short fiction market. This revelation

That unfinished novel...

was like a prospector finding a large vein of gold. The prospector would work the vein until it was exhausted. I worked the vein of baseball writing successfully for the next twenty years.

I chose to stop writing fiction about ten years ago, partly because of the market conditions. For example, my novel *Box Socials* sold about 70,000 hardcover copies, but when the sequel was ready the publisher not only didn't want to publish it; they didn't want to read it. Not enough sales. Go figure!

Short stories were out of fashion again, and the market for non-trash novels was shrinking monthly. Besides, I had said about all I had to say, and I have seen far too many writers scribbling on into their old age. Updike, Mailer and Anne Tyler come to mind, turning out inferior and repetitious parodies of their earlier brilliant work.

I have drawn criticism for touting myself as a professional writer whose income should match that of other professionals such as doctors, lawyers or engineers. I have no time for the "writer living in a garret mentality," with art coming first and income second. Book sales have always been the bottom line with me. A manuscript is nothing until it is published; a published book is nothing unless it is widely read.

In that vein, I'll close with a favourite epigram from Hilaire Belloc: "When I am dead, I hope it may be said: 'His sins were scarlet, but his books were read.'"

[2009]

Look Back in Laughter

ꜱ ERIC NICOL

■ A three-time recipient of the Leacock Medal for Humour, Eric Nicol
contributed a humour column to the *Vancouver Province* for fifty years and
has published more than thirty books. In the essay that follows, he remarks
on the uniquely British Columbian experiences and exposures that make
West Coasters so much funnier than all other Canadians. Alas, not everyone
on this side of the Rockies has a fully developed funny bone; Nicol remarks
on the all-too-serious politicos and public figures who are driving away the
endangered Funnyman. Essentially, one of BC's best known humorists offers
a survival guide for everyone else to try to cut their teeth on jokes. Eric Nicol
died in Vancouver at the age of ninety-one, on February 2, 2011.

A QUESTION I'M OFTEN ASKED: "Do you think you could have survived as a professional humorist if you hadn't lived in British Columbia?"
(Actually, I've never been asked that question, but it is more useful here
than "Where's the men's room?")

Answer: No. I'm sure my inhabiting BC has been absolutely essential
to hacking it — if that is the gerund I want — as a professional humorist.

BC teems with humorists. Most of them don't even know they are funny. They go into politics, get chosen as party leaders, and regularly are elected to become the provincial premier. I have been told that Canadian humorists have been sighted east of the Rockies, but so have UFOs. It has been years since the late Bob Edwards was seen around Calgary. Paul Hiebert, the rogue professor who roamed over *Sarah Binks*, was a literary aberration, never repeated in Manitoba. Stephen Leacock was the last of the Ontario hoots. A freak body of water — Brewery Bay — near Orillia favoured the deviant academic that was Leacock.

Climate plays a role. BC's wild herds of humorists are able to feed one-liners all year round. Vancouver abounds in comedy clubs that provide shelter, if not forage, for monologists of both sexes. The rutting season for comedy extends from early January to late December.

But the factor most conducive to BC humour is the topography of the province. In particular, the mountains. It is impossible, for me at least, to live in the immediate presence of the Coast Range without being imbued with a sense of the ridiculous, as an object only five feet ten inches high.

The noblest work of God? Gimme a break. Grouse Mountain — *there's* his heavyweight. I once tried to challenge Grouse on skis. Grouse won. I got a humour piece out of the humiliation. That is how BC works, for the humorist. She or he has relations with a mountain, or the Pacific Ocean, ends up lost in a canyon, or marooned on an island, and garners enough grist for milling into a 1,000-word piece for the Sunday supplement.

A writer can't get the same effect from the CN Tower. If Torontonians have a problem with levity — as indeed they do — it is because they can see no natural feature to persuade them that they are not necessarily the lords of creation. This explains why Torontonians experience laughter as an acquired trait.

Regrettably, laughter in Vancouver is, like good fresh air to breathe, diminishing with the spread of political correctitude. More and more journalists writing for the city's mainstream media are starting to take themselves seriously — a grievous affliction. They turn up for work sober. They join trade unions.

Unions! Attending just one union-members' meeting can zap one's sense of humour. I have felt obliged to join various writers' unions in my time, but now always with the tacit understanding that I would *never* attend a meeting, or call someone "brother" or "sister" simply because we are linked by greed.

So, many BC humorists have taken to the woods. They live off berries and *Raincoast Chronicles*. The Sunshine Coast is a virtual humorists' refuge. Or they migrate to the Gulf Islands, where their loonish laughter blends with the raven's cackle. Some, those who affect the straw sucked between the teeth, find a congenial field up the Fraser Valley, and grow beans beside a reasonable facsimile of Walden Pond, till the RCMP come and drag it for a body.

That is the problem for the BC humorist: being forced, by the pressure of urban sprawl, farther and farther into the wilderness, to avoid being contaminated by organization. Some funny folk are said to be locating as far north as the Arctic Circle. They read their humour pieces to sled dogs, and eventually become totally mad, though happy with it. What does this mean for the future of the professional humorist in British Columbia? As a specimen rapidly becoming of interest only to literary anthropologists, I would say: Keep your day job. Get online with the Internet and engage your rapier wit in a duel with another amateur humorist, in some outback where editors are eaten alfresco.

Who knows, you may build up an international audience and eventual fame, without ever seeing a word of yours in print. Frankly, I prefer to lodge between hard covers, but much depends on the stamina of the BC forests that supply the paper. It's a dilemma: hug a tree, or Talonbooks? Tough call.

[1995]

Laughter Is the Best Sports Medicine

ᴖ JIM TAYLOR

■ Jim Taylor was once BC's most widely read sports columnist. He drank beer
from the Stanley Cup, saw Paul Henderson score "The Goal" in 1972, and he
once predicted rookie place-kicker Lui Passaglia — who became the all-time
top scorer in professional football — wouldn't last with the BC Lions more
than one season. Along the way he wrote more than 8,000 newspaper
columns. In the following essay, Taylor discusses the necessity of humour
in the practice of sports reporting.

WHEN I LEFT THE sports pages for good in 2001, I swore not to become
one of those tiresome carping old farts who bitch at the way things are
and long for the days that were. I'd like a mulligan on that. Just a little
one.

I need to know where the laughter went.

The weekly crop of fiscal foolishness, fat-headed owners, tunnel-
visioned executives and jockstrap me-firsters has never been more boun-
tiful. Yet I see little laughter in the sports sections. It's not that there's no
one who could do it. There are gifted young writers out there, sharp and
sardonic and fully capable of inserting needles in the hides of the pompous

or poking fun at silly masquerading as important. But somewhere between press box cynicism and laptop creativity they sip the cliché Kool-Aid and slide the sabre back into the sheath. I'm not sure why. Maybe, in this new mixed-media universe, management doesn't want it. Were I still with one of the Vancouver dailies I doubt I'd be allowed to lambaste Vancouver's 2010 Olympics bid, that monument to excess and misguided enthusiasm, as I would have from the day the bid was announced.

In a city where the media race to see who can over-cover the Vancouver Canucks has turned into a year-long preoccupation, there might not be room for a guy who looked at the old black, orange and yellow uniforms and suggested they looked like there should be a candle under every helmet, and that the huge V was on the front of the jersey to point them to where they were to put on the jockstraps.

Well, *of course* I'm biased. I made a living laughing. Mind you, I was blessed with editors who let me run even as they wondered what the Lone Ranger was doing in a sports column; or what the hell I was doing writing about riding an elephant in Thailand and telling our guide that in North America all elephants were named Gerald in honour of the great jazz singer Elephants Gerald. Or why I demanded that Disney president Michael Eisner explain, as his company created the NHL's Anaheim Mighty Ducks, how a family-oriented business could let Donald Duck care for his three underage nephews when he had no visible means of employment and they were all running around without pants.

But early in the game I learned an important lesson: people like to laugh. If you can amuse them as you make your point there's a better chance they'll see it, or at least read to the end. The other half of the equation: When you stop laughing, when you really get ticked about something, rear back and throw the high hard one, it has even more impact.

[2009]

Earle's Girls

—◦ A.T.

■ When Earle Birney was still alive, institutionalized at age ninety as an invalid and unable to fight back, Elspeth Cameron's comprehensive, 512-page biography, *Earle Birney: A Life* (Penguin), was viewed by some as a cold-blooded act of premature literary cannibalism.

THERE IS AMPLE evidence that Earle Birney gave lasting satisfaction to an astonishing parade of women — he appears to have been, believe it or not, a great Canadian lover — but in *Earle Birney: A Life*, Elspeth Cameron dwells on the pain Birney caused, rarely the pleasure he apparently gave.

Cameron stops short of describing Birney as a foolish old lecher — but she and long-suffering Esther Birney (who describes her ex-husband as "the most irascible man that mortal woman was ever tormented with") clearly resent that an elderly man could continue to bed and apparently satisfy young and exotic women while in his seventies and eighties.

Cameron says she saw Earle Birney as a conqueror of women in a dream she had in 1991. She has taken this "dreamed-up" interpretation seriously. Birney is compared to Loki ("greedy, selfish and treacherous") and Don Quixote ("the spindly old white-bearded knight tilting at windmills").

As well, Birney is presented as a mama's boy, an adolescent pervert, a faithless husband, a reluctant father and a clever schemer whose ambition outstripped his talent. The result is a fascinating and probably controversial study of a highly successful, messy life — a landmark in the much-too-thin canon of British Columbia belles lettres. Only Ben Metcalfe's controversial and largely banished 1985 biography of Roderick Haig-Brown, *A Man of Some Importance*, comes remotely close to matching Cameron's book in terms of providing an in-depth look at the incestuous and sometimes nasty world of BC literature.

"The history of the development of contemporary writing in Vancouver, from 1946 to 1960," Birney once noted, "is pretty largely a one-man show, and that man was me."

Cameron proves him right. By the 1950s, by his own count, Earle Birney had corresponded with 1,200 people on seven continents. A gifted Chaucer scholar and passionate Trotskyite in the 1930s, he later founded Canada's first full-fledged Creative Writing Department at the University of British Columbia, bringing in Robert Harlow as the first department head. He wrote one of Canada's most famous poems ("David"), received two Governor General's Awards, and befriended nearly every major Canadian writer for five decades, while inspiring and supporting literally dozens of younger writers.

Unfortunately, Elspeth Cameron displays little or no empathy for her subject. After her biographies of the genteel Hugh MacLennan and the bombastic Irving Layton, Cameron has managed to dissect and reduce another male with all the grace of a lepidopterist sticking pins in butterflies. When Cameron asks, "could Birney really empathize with anyone but himself?" the reader wonders if this is a case of the pot calling the kettle black.

Earle Birney was born in Calgary on May 13, 1904. He was then raised as an only child on a remote ten-acre bush farm. He later moved to Banff and Creston with his working-class parents. "I was constantly being rejected by the group because I was no bloody good in team sports," he declared.

Birney was apparently a condescending know-it-all, a social climber and something of a sissy. The lanky, carrot-headed teen ("dazed with lust") rejected a banking career in Vernon and headed for the brothel to be deflowered at age seventeen. Participating in UBC's Great Trek in 1922, he enrolled at UBC where he was encouraged by the Harvard-educated mentor, Garnett Sedgewick who, Cameron suggests, was a homosexual. Sedgewick ushered the awkward Birney towards academe.

Following a stint as the editor of *The Ubyssey* newspaper in 1925, Birney received his masters degree from the University of Toronto, studied at Berkeley, taught at the University of Utah in 1930, and returned to the University of Toronto in 1933, where he met Dorothy Livesay — a Stalinist. Half a century later, Livesay would falsely assert that Birney's much-anthologized poem about a mountain-climbing death, "David," was autobiographical and Birney was, in effect, a murderer. Untrue.

During the '30s in Vancouver, Toronto and Utah, Birney became a party organizer for the Trotskyite branch of the Communist Party. After going to England to study Chaucer at the British Museum, Birney went to Norway and interviewed his political hero, Leon Trotsky, in 1936. More significantly he met Esther Heiger, of Russian-Jewish descent, who served as his stenographer. The idealistic pair lived like gypsies in Dorset where Esther, recently divorced, helped him complete his 860-page thesis on Chaucer's irony.

After moving to Vancouver, Esther shared a house with Earle Birney's Presbyterian mother in Vancouver before the unwed couple moved to Toronto. Expecting the birth of their only son, Bill, in 1940, Birney broke with Trotskyism and obtained a marriage license.

"We got married for the sole purpose of giving the child legitimacy," Esther Birney recalls, "We both thought marriage was a bourgeois institution having to do with property and possessions. We had a Marxist beginning and set out to live according to *The Communist Manifesto*. We believed you don't possess people. For this reason, neither of us objected to affairs."

Birney then escaped to war. A negligent father, he enlisted at age thirty-nine to serve overseas as a training officer. Later he would refashion his military experiences into a satirical novel, *Turvey* (1949). This was followed by a memoir/novel of his Trotskyite days, *Down the Long Table* (1955). In the post-war years he was celebrated as "the soldier poet." His first poetry collection, *David and Other Poems*, earned a Governor General's Award, as did his second collection, *Now is Time*.

Birney began aggressively climbing the academic ladder, jostling for power at UBC with Roy Daniells, helped by Garnett Sedgewick ("the man of all men who has stood nearest in the role of father to me"), developing relations with Deep Cove's Malcolm Lowry and Bowen Island's Einar Neilson and learning how to obtain grants with remarkable skill.

Birney knew everyone worth knowing: Lister Sinclair, E.J. Pratt, Louis Dudek, Lorne Pierce, Alan Crawley, Ralph Gustafson, Clyde Gilmour, Fred Cogswell, F.R. Scott, John Adaskin, Norrie Frye, Dal Grauer, Vincent Massey, Claude Bissell, Morley Callaghan, Robert Weaver, Jack Shadbolt, Anne Marriot, Roderick Haig-Brown, Bill McConnell, P.K. Page, Ethel Wilson, Paul Engle, Miriam Waddington, Kaye Lamb, Jack McClelland, Irving Layton, Luis Bunuel, Leonard Cohen and Stephen Vizinczey — to name a few.

According to Cameron, he also began affairs with many of his most gifted female students, such as Phyllis Webb, Betty Lambert and Rona Murray. Throughout his life he was sexually active with countless women despite his demanding literary and academic careers. In fact, there are so many significant lovers mentioned in Cameron's biography that the reader simply begins to lose track. A large percentage of Birney's lovers remained intimate friends for decades. "I know full well that I brought genuine love to those women, which is still with them and which they draw strength from to this day," he wrote.

The many students that Birney directly helped include Jack Hodgins ("the fact that he existed caused me to want to be good"), Tom Wayman, Daryl Duke, and Norm Klenman (founders of CKUV), Heather Spears, George Bowering, Norman Newton, Frank Davey, George Johnston, Bill Galt, Lionel Kearns, Mary McAlpine, Daphne Marlatt, Ernie Perrault, and Robert Harlow.

Birney organized Vancouver visits by Dylan Thomas, Theodore Roethke and W.H. Auden. He obtained teaching positions for George Woodcock. He helped establish *Canadian Literature* and *Prism international*. And he supported Michael Ondaatje, David Cronenberg, bill bissett (whose *blewointmentpress* he considered "the only genuinely experimental/contemporary mag in Canada"), Austin Clarke, John Robert Colombo, Gwendolyn MacEwen, Joe Rosenblatt, John Newlove and Al Purdy — to name a few.

He was homophobic, cantankerous, self-righteous, vain; he loved fast cars and travel, but his influence was unparalleled. Birney wrote the most famous poem about Vancouver ("The Damnation of Vancouver"). He was committed to internationalism ("Canada has a chance to be a great independent force for the pacification of the world"). And, as a Canadian on the UBC English faculty, he resisted American cultural imperialism ("By god we've got to stand up and say we aren't Yanks and won't necessarily ever be Yanks").

To his credit or discredit, Birney tried to change with the times, wearing Nehru jackets and participating in protests. He went on a reading tour with Irving Layton and Leonard Cohen and realized that Cohen was superior. He mixed poetry with live jazz. He experimented with concrete poetry. But he had more difficulty accepting the TISH movement at UBC. "They introduced cultism in its extreme form," he later wrote, "Anything written unlike what they were writing was dubbed not just inferior, but anti-poetry. How the Puritan mind is reborn in every new movement!"

In 1964 Birney brought home a twenty-four-year-old art student and poet, Ikuko Atusmi. "I've had a lot of crazy and perilous amorous adventures in my life," he confided to Irving Layton, "95 percent of them unknown to anybody but the girl concerned — but this turmoil I'm in now is farther out than a Burroughs novel. . . . I'm going through the greatest, most beautiful and, no kidding, most passionate sexual experience of my life and I've no complaints about the past ones." Birney left Esther — again — but when Ikuko suddenly left for Japan, Esther allowed him back in 1966.

In 1973, after his heart attack at age sixty-nine, Birney began cohabiting with a beautiful, twenty-four-year-old Cantonese graduate student,

Wailin (Lily) Low. This became Birney's greatest love affair. After Birney suffered a near-fatal fall while climbing a tree in July of 1975 — at age seventy-one — Wailin lovingly nursed him back to health and revitalized his spirits and his writing. She also remained at his side after his near-fatal heart attack in 1987. She continues as his protectress, allegedly resentful of Cameron's frank biography (which she had initially supported).

The rapturous liaison with Wailin led to Birney's divorce from Esther in 1977. Birney was generous with property settlements. The grounds for divorce were adultery. The papers specifically noted there had been no sexual relationship between Earle and Esther Birney for the previous fifteen years.

The thirty-seven-year marriage between Earle and Esther Birney must rank as one of the most unusual in the history of Canadian letters. Esther often referred to Earle Birney as a goat and joked about his large penis. At the same time she felt bitterly betrayed by him and horrified by her habitual partnership. "What kind of de-sexed mouse was I — to burn & suffer & go on. . . . Don't torture me by telling me I am 'always with you' that I am always your loved Esther. I'm not. I am your deserted, lied to, unloved Esther & I have been for years, since you came home from the war."

For his part, Birney equated creativity with virility. "I don't want to equate art with sexual infidelity but in me there must be a connection somewhere. There is some deeply rooted thing in me that not only desires other women's bodies, but that makes me spill over with very genuine feelings of tenderness and affection for more than one woman. . . . I think loving is also a philosophy and kind of substitute art."

Birney once summed himself up succinctly in a poem. It ended self-mockingly: "too large an ego and too small a head / a sheep in company and a goat in bed." At the time when Cameron's biography of Birney appeared, BC's most seminal literary figure and most important poet was still clinging to the edge of his mountainous ego, marooned as a difficult patient at Toronto's Queen Elizabeth Hospital — refusing to butt out.

[1994]

A Trip Down Nightmare Alley

⟶ CHUCK DAVIS

■ Chuck Davis, congenial radio host, quizmaster, newspaper columnist and author, devoted his life to being the expert on the city of Vancouver's history and its environs. His first landmark volume, *The Vancouver Book* (1976), for which he was listed as general editor, was long regarded as his foremost accomplishment, even though it was eclipsed in size by his 882-page omnibus, *The Greater Vancouver Book* (1997), co-produced with business partner John Cochlin. Davis' unfortunate choice to self-publish the latter was what denied him commercial success. Here Davis recalls in candid and humble detail the self-inflicted self-publishing detour that led him from Easy Street to Nightmare Alley.

SOMETHING STRANGE HAPPENED to me on the morning I started writing this. I was reading Deena Rosenberg's book *Fascinating Rhythm*, about George and Ira Gershwin. It describes the piano in the centre of the room, one of George's favourite Steinway grands, where the brothers wrote all the songs from *Porgy and Bess*. I imagined standing in that room, awestruck, when suddenly and alarmingly I found myself blinking back tears.

I put the book aside, swallowing repeatedly to erase that ugly and unexpected little spasm of self-pity. The vision of the Gershwin brothers excitedly moving around that piano, George humming and playing new melodies, Ira creating those wonderfully smart lyrics, both men jauntily writing down their work, contrasted so painfully with my own agony of recent years, trying to create while eaten by worry and fear.

For four years I have been in the middle of a financial nightmare, caused by my creation of a book — my thirteenth — called *The Greater Vancouver Book*. That book drove my partner into personal bankruptcy, created an instant army of angry unpaid contributors, and saddled me with a debt. I have been paying off that debt at an average of about $500 a week and I will be paying for many years to come. That debt takes every cent I make, and I survive only because of my loving, generous (and steadily working) wife of thirty-six years.

I've asked her not to read this article if it runs. It would be just too damned painful.

How did a project that was going to put us on Easy Street dump us instead into Nightmare Alley? How did I come to have unpaid contributors snubbing me on the street, threatening to sue, and writing us nasty letters, including an anonymous "Merry Christmas" greeting scrawled on a piece of used toilet paper?

Return with me to 1993. I was working on *Top Dog!*, the history of CKNW. When that work was finished, immeasurably faster thanks to the computer assistance of John and Kathy McQuarrie, we talked about a possible new project. Out of that discussion came the decision to launch *The Greater Vancouver Book*.

I had wanted for years to expand my 1976 *Vancouver Book*, an "urban almanac." Every time I walked into Duthie's, the staff would ask when I was going to do an update. The book sold out, but the publisher (J.J. Douglas, now Douglas & McIntyre) declined to produce more because it had been too costly and time-consuming for them. I should have remembered that.

Even at 500 big pages, I thought *The Vancouver Book* was too small. My inclination was, and remains, to get *everything* in. I even toyed, but only briefly, with the idea of including maps showing every building in the city. And I mean every building. I'm not entirely sane about stuff like this. My first major decision was that every article in the new book would be brand new and at least 1.5 times bigger than in the original, more subjects would be included, and the area covered would be not just the city but all of Greater Vancouver. Because of its size and expanded coverage, we'd call it an "urban encyclopedia."

Denny Boyd had been a fan of the original, *The Vancouver Book*. He was tickled when I told him that back in 1976 *TVB* had been the second most frequently stolen book in the Vancouver Public Library system. "What," Denny wanted to know, "was the first most-stolen book?" It was *Mein Kampf*, by Adolf Hitler. Denny said, "Thank God the *other* guy isn't planning a sequel."

I rashly announced I would write the entire book myself. It soon became apparent that wouldn't work. I could do it, but it would take way too long. We'd calculated the project would take two and a half years. With more than 200 contributors, it ended up taking four. So we needed more writers. How to pay them? Sponsorships, I said. There would be no advertising in the book, but pages and sections could be sponsored. We'd put what's called "institutional" copy along the bottom of sponsored pages.

My very first cold call resulted in sponsorship of the back cover by BC Gas! An old friend, adman Fin Anthony, advised me to double our fee schedule for everything. We discovered to our delight, it made absolutely no difference. Sponsorships continued to pile up. We ended up with more than 200 sponsors. Many major companies signed on: Air Canada, BC Rail, BC Hydro, Canfor, VanCity, Finning, the Pan Pacific Hotel. I never got cocky but I was supremely confident that John and I were going to produce a blockbuster. By the end, Fin and I sold more than $300,000 in sponsorships.

But a small cloud was beginning to form.

The cost of the paper went up $40,000 *while the book was in production*. We were able to work out a *contra* deal with the paper company. But other costs of the book were rising steadily, far beyond what we'd expected. We could have saved thousands of dollars having the book printed in Hong Kong, but I said, "Hey, we can't celebrate Greater Vancouver with a book printed in Hong Kong." Gawd, I was stupid.

Payment for these hard, practical things began to make it difficult to pay our contributors. The book couldn't happen without production work, without paper and printing, so we had to give these items priority. We gave advances to many of our earlier writers, but then we started asking others to do the work on promise of payment.

This was the thirteenth book I'd written, co-written or edited, but it was the first I'd ever published. To make a long and ugly story short, the total cost of the project was about $700,000 or so, meaning we were short about $400,000 from breaking even. The book would have to sell really well to make that up. We were sure it would.

The articles by our 200-plus writers — more than twenty of whom, by the way, had also contributed to the 1976 book — covered just about every aspect of life in metropolitan Vancouver. Their work was extensive, and fact-filled and (my favourite description of the book) useful. Constance Brissenden, for instance, worked for months on her list of 500 people of Greater Vancouver's past. At 47,000 words, it's a small book in itself. Nothing like it has ever been done before, and I'm prouder of her work in the book than I am about any other writer's.

The book ended up a big, fat, fact-packed marvel. Late as it was, we were very proud of it. The first copies came out of the bindery on June 11, 1997.

The first review appeared in the *Sun*: the book was trashed. Thoroughly. The reviewer hated the articles, hated the cover, hated the paper it was printed on, she didn't like this and didn't like that, and on and on and on. It was a complete slash-and-burn job. Except for one thing: She had a kind word for Shane McCune's article on Burn's Bog.

I handled the distribution of the book, so I knew the *Sun* reviewer had had it for less than a week, maybe about two days. It's a book of more than 800,000 words, seven or eight times the size of a standard novel. That review was a body blow. The *Province* didn't review the book but they did run a photo of me holding it, with a nice caption. A little while later, the *Sun*'s City Limits column asked if they could run the occasional little tidbit from the book for free, in return for credit to the source. I agreed. CBC Radio's Ira Nadel gave it a terrific plug. I still recall listening to it, and saying, "Thank you, Ira!"

We'd tried to interest *Business in Vancouver* in our project because it was financed by local businesses, but the magazine never wrote a story. Then one day, after our real financial problems had started, we got a call from one of *Business in Vancouver*'s writers, who said he'd heard the book was in trouble. *Now* they were interested. I was so angry I could never bring myself to read whatever they printed.

Still blinded by our prospects for the book, John and I sent out letters time and again telling our contributors they would eventually be paid. And time and time again we just couldn't do it. Many times over these past four years I've received mail from writers that I didn't have the heart, or the guts, to open, and phone messages I found difficult or impossible to reply to.

The book did sell well but — in yet another example of my doltishness — I had arranged for 20,000 to be printed. At the full retail price of $39.95, that would be $799,000. Deduct the 40 percent bookstore commission ($319,600) and that would leave us with $479,400. Add the sponsorships to get approximately $779,000, deduct the $700,000 cost of the project and John/Kathy and I would split the hypothetical $79,000 net. That would be $39,500 to each of the partners for the work of four years, a little under $10,000 a year. Not quite enough for my dreamed-of four-door XJ6 Jaguar sedan.

In the end, we sold, not 20,000, but 11,000, with a couple thousand of those at a discount, all in one corner of the country. In terms of sales, *The Greater Vancouver Book* was a roaring success. But thanks to that "success," John and I found ourselves in debt about a quarter of a million dollars. Visions of Samarkand and Machu Picchu faded, to be replaced by a sea of outstretched hands.

The biggest hand belonged to the bank, from which we had made a big loan to cover the unanticipated extra costs of producing the book. The second biggest was attached to the credit union at which I had arranged, for the same purpose, a second mortgage on our home. The most stressful fact in all of this mess is that I had no one else to blame.

I had met the enemy and he was me.

I vividly recall a night back in 1998 when I waited for the decision of the judges as to which book would win the City of Vancouver Book Award that year. I *really* wanted to win that award and the $1,000 that went with it. *The Greater Vancouver Book* did win, and the very next morning I rushed to the credit union with that $1,000 cheque, just in time to pay my mortgage.

With three kids to support, and besieged on all sides by creditors, John had to make a decision. He declared personal bankruptcy. Goodbye to family trips to Disneyland. (He's out of bankruptcy now and doing well in unrelated work. And, astonishingly, he and I are still friends. In fact, we've just produced an offshoot called *Vancouver Then and Now*.)

I decided not to go into bankruptcy because I *knew* virtually all of those writers. I didn't want to go through what's left of my life having to look aside in embarrassment when I met one of them. I've been told I could have declared bankruptcy, got some relief, and still paid them off down the road. But I just couldn't do it.

Just before I started writing this article, an event occurred that convinced me it had to be written. It was Wednesday night, September 5, at a Bard on the Beach performance of *Taming of the Shrew* (for which we had complimentary tickets). One of the book's contributors was also in the audience, and when our eyes happened to meet there was a little flash of anger and contempt from her. What was painful about that particular occasion was that she was one of the really good writers, and had sent me a letter shortly before beginning her assignments complimenting me on the pay scale I had set. We offered writers an average of about $400 a page. Contrast that with the payment I got for writing three articles in the *Canadian Encyclopedia*: $45. Total. That is not a misprint.

As a writer myself, one who has often been paid less than the work warranted, I wanted to do the decent thing. Now that angry writer is still waiting four years later for her money. She has lots of company. How many other contributors are out there, convinced we made a killing on the book?

Some of the writers, knowing my financial situation, wrote me to say, forget what I owe them. Such generous and compassionate responses are gratefully acknowledged, and will be resolutely ignored. I commissioned the work, they did they work, and I'll pay for it. I would expect nothing less from someone who owed *me* money.

I still await the day I can start sending out letters that begin, "Please find enclosed a cheque for . . ."

[2002]

Ten Commandments from Two Peerless Freelancers

⌐ PIERRE BERTON & PETER NEWMAN

■ Pierre Berton cut his teeth as a reporter in Vancouver and headed east. Peter Newman temporarily lived on a berth at Grantham's Landing on the Sunshine Coast. Both were friendly supporters of *BC BookWorld*. They happily contributed the following advice on freelance writing.

Peter Newman: The Peter Principles

1. Thou shalt never forget that you're not writing to please yourself, your editor or your publisher — but your reader.
2. Thou shalt never give up. Your first book will be the hardest.
3. Thou shalt read your manuscript aloud to a sympathetic listener. (Thou shalt be amazed by how many writing errors can be picked up through this simple process.)
4. Thou shalt pay no attention to reviewers. They are butchers on a mission that has nothing to do with the quality of your prose.

5. Thou shalt try to write by using your gut as much as your brain —
   because feelings are always more compelling than thoughts.

Pierre Berton: The Pierre Principles

1. Thou shalt write only the kind of book that you yourself would purchase at once if you found it on the shelf of a bookstore.
2. Thou shalt never start a book without giving yourself a series of deadlines. Work out the date you want the book published, work back from
   that.
3. Thou shalt not send manuscripts to friends asking for opinions. They
   are almost as useless to you as critics.
4. Thou shalt rewrite, rewrite, rewrite. Some paragraphs should be rewritten thirteen or fourteen times.
5. Thou shalt be prepared to give up things. If you're not making your
   deadlines, then don't go to the movies, watch television or take in the
   opera. Or even drink with your buddies.

[1999]

Vicarious narcissim

Who's *Not* Afraid of
Virginia Woolf?

‑o MEG TILLY

■ With four titles under her belt, former Hollywood star Meg Tilley has a
growing reputation as a novelist — her young adult novel *Porcupine* (Tundra
2007) was nominated for a BC Book Prize. But life is about taking risks, and
in the essay that follows, Tilley describes how and why, in 2011, she decided
to revisit her acting career by taking the starring role as Martha in Edward
Albee's *Who's Afraid of Virginia Woolf?* at Victoria's McPherson Playhouse.
Although Oscar-nominated Tilley appeared in films such as *The Big Chill*
and *Agnes of God*, this was her first appearance in live theatre.

WOULD ANYONE IN THEIR right mind volunteer to memorize a hefty
two-hundred-and-fifty-seven pages of dialogue, then exacerbate the situation by not only agreeing to rattle off said two-hundred-and-fifty-seven
pages of material while trying to climb into the skin of an incredibly
complicated woman, but agreeing to do it under bright lights, on a nightly
basis, in a theatre full of hundreds of strangers?

I don't know the answer to that question. I do know that not only did

I agree to play Martha in Edward Albee's *Who's Afraid of Virginia Woolf?* but I really, *really* wanted to do it. And the question that hovers above me, circling like an unwieldy turkey vulture, day after day, as I try to cram all these lines into my fifty-one-year-old premenopausal brain, is: *why?*

I wish I had a simple answer for you, but I don't. It was a mishmash of events that led me to this point. My youngest child left home last year and after spending the last twenty-six years of my life raising, cooking, supporting and loving my three kids, when the house emptied, there was a hole.

I write novels, but even that was no longer enough. I found myself getting up from my desk after spending hours alone, hunched over my keyboard, staring at a glowing screen, and thinking to myself, as I stretched the kinks out of my back, that just writing wasn't sufficient anymore. That if plugging out another manuscript and another, and another, was all that I did to the end of my days, I would have squandered too many of life's precious hours.

I made an effort to contact old friends, to try to make new ones. I started going on long walks, trying to absorb the smells of the woods, the cold slap of salty ocean-scented air, the crunch and slide of pebbles under my feet, smoothed out from being tossed on countless shores, and it was good. It did help, but still it wasn't enough.

And then, this Christmas, after the hustle and bustle of stockings and presents and turkey dinner, after my sisters had left and my visiting children had disappeared to their various corners of the house, I bent over to switch off the Christmas tree lights and I found a small wrapped present that had been overlooked sitting forlornly under the tree. "A present!" I said, dropping to my belly, so I could reach under the branches and rescue it.

It was for me! *For Meg,* was on the gift tag and *love, Jennifer* was scrawled underneath. And there was something magical about finding that present in the darkened living room, the house quiet, the Christmas tree lights twinkling. There was something about holding that small little box in my hand that caused a tingle to go chasing through me.

I went to my writing room, shut the door, sat at my desk and carefully unwrapped it. Inside, nestled on a bed of cotton was a silver bracelet.

"Hmm . . ." I said. There was something carved on the thin band. I held it closer so I could see more clearly. *It is never too late to be what you might have been* — a George Eliot quote.

Oh pooh, I thought, sitting back in my chair, the bracelet resting on my upturned palms. That's silly. I am very happy with my life. And right on the heels of that, *You've always wanted to do theatre*, dropped into my head. Instantly, I was scared. Scared, but excited, because I knew there was no going back. One thing led to another, and within a matter of weeks I found myself committed to performing in *Who's Afraid of Virginia Woolf?*, this July, at the McPherson Playhouse.

I vacillate between being thrilled and totally terrified. Would I go back and undo it? Absolutely not! And yes, I might make a total fool of myself, fall on my ass or worse, but whatever happens, good or bad, at least I won't die with regrets on my lips, disappointed in myself, that I had this secret dream and I didn't even try.

[2011]

George Woodcock: A Tribute

⟿ ROBIN SKELTON

■ As Robin Skelton points out, a "Man of Letters" is one who is a writer,
scholar and critic who "[cannot] reasonably be listed under only one
heading." Himself a poet, anthologist, editor, teacher, biographer, art and
literary critic, historical writer, initiated witch and occultist, and founder of
The Malahat Review, Skelton fits his own definition of a Man of Letters,
thus making him qualified to bestow the title upon others.

GEORGE WOODCOCK IS Canada's leading Man of Letters. Originally
the term "Man of Letters" meant learned man. Later it grew to mean a
scholar and writer, and later still a writer who, as well as being a scholar
and critic, was also proficient in a number of other genres, an author who
could not reasonably be listed under only one heading.

Over the centuries only a small number of people have been called Men
or Women of Letters largely because of lack of opportunity for such di-
versity. We must, however, give Samuel Johnson the title for being a poet,
fiction writer, essayist, biographer and lexicographer. Oliver Goldsmith
also deserves the title. If we do, indeed, think of the term as a title, as an

honorific, then the number of candidates for the position dwindles and in the twentieth century perhaps G.K. Chesterton is one of the few certainties, though his range is not as wide as that of George Woodcock who may, indeed, be the most fully qualified for the label of any writer in English.

This may seem a vast claim, but the headings for George Woodcock's more than 120 books prove the point. Poetry, plays, memoirs and letters, literary criticism, essays, art, history, travel, biography, politics, translations, symposia, anthologies, scholarly editions — all are represented, together with that immensely significant contribution to our sense of ourselves, the quarterly, *Canadian Literature*, which he helped to establish in 1959 and edited for eighteen years.

A great many of George Woodcock's books are essential reading; I would instance his works on George Orwell, William Godwin and Aphra Behn, and his many contributions to the exploration of Anarchism and to the study of Canadian history and Canadian writing. His industry is as astonishing as his humility; he has never turned away from a task because it lacked obvious importance, but he has performed the most menial of writers' tasks with the same enlightened efficiency as he has tackled the major challenges.

George Woodcock is a very great Man of Letters, and he is more than that. He is a National Treasure and in a properly constituted society his eightieth birthday would have been celebrated with the issuing of a postage stamp, the striking of a medal, and a burst of cannon fire on Parliament Hill.

[1994]

On Receiving the Freedom of the City

―ഗ GEORGE WOODCOCK

■ George Woodcock died on January 28, 1995, less than one year after receiving the Freedom of the City of Vancouver, the highest award given by the city. In the chambers of city council, George Woodcock delivered the following speech about his relationship with Vancouver and the honour he felt at receiving the award as well as its significance with regards to the evolution of the city as a literary centre.

IN THE EARLY 1950s when my wife and I were living in frustrated isolation in a small Vancouver Island village, Jack and Doris Shadbolt suggested we should come to live in Vancouver. At that time Capitol Hill, where Jack and Doris lived, was mainly bush, and Jack suggested that he might get us the loan of a cabin there, which he did, and our life on the mainland began in a stretch of woodland, now long vanished, where the pheasants still called and the tanagers still nested.

A couple of years later we moved into the city proper, and my wife and I have now lived here for more than forty years. Vancouver has become the foundation of our lives. We have travelled far and often, but through it all Vancouver has remained the magic and magnetic centre of our world. We love the city and its setting, the mountains and the sea and the trees and flowers, we have found our place in its special way of life, and in Vancouver I have done most of my life's work of writing.

That surely is debt enough for me to declare. But now, with the Freedom of the City and the Freedom Medal, I am being incorporated into the community in a special and intimate way, and I am grateful.

But beyond my own personal satisfaction, I see a special, broader, implicit meaning in my having been the first writer to be named a Freeman of the City of Vancouver. I see it as a tribute also to our flourishing literary community, in the same way as granting Freedom to Jack Shadbolt a few years before was a recognition of the visual arts as well as of Jack himself.

When I first came to Vancouver in the early 1950s it was a lonely place with few fellow writers, with no publishers, and with one slender poetry magazine, Alan Crawley's *Contemporary Verse*. Now Vancouver is the centre of a province inhabited by hundreds of professional writers, with scores of publishing houses large and small, and many literary magazines, some of them with national and even international reputations. It poses

Deafness

The new radical

a growing rivalry to the older literary centres of Eastern Canada. This is a matter for rejoicing, and I am glad, ladies and gentlemen, that you have recognized it through honouring me.

I have still something on my mind. Freedom! It is a word worth repeating, for what I have been given is by definition a Freedom medal, and the great role of cities in the development of our ideals and practice of freedom has not always been recognized, or fully understood. The very words, civil rights, civil behaviour, and civilization itself, derive from one Latin root, *civitas* — which the scholars call "kivitas" — meaning the city. Even before the Romans, two and a half millennia ago, our concepts of democratic life were being sketched out and tested in the free cities of ancient Greece.

But the honour you have given me belongs to a later period and shows how consistently, over the ages, cities have cared for freedom. In the Middle Ages the merchants and artisans of Europe created their own free cities on the seacoasts and river banks of the feudal world. People who lived outside the cities were mostly vassals and serfs of lords or kings. People in the cities carried on their trade and their industries, and practised their arts in free co-operation and defended themselves through their guilds and fraternities. And when a serf fleeing from a tyrannical landlord found his way through the city gate and was accepted, he became a free man in name and practice.

I see this association of the city and mental and physical freedom as an important, valuable tradition, not to be lost. I see myself as the symbolic descendant of that fleeing serf, and that is why I feel such pleasure at becoming a Freeman of my own city of Vancouver.

[1994]

Potpourri

Scary Reds

✐ SHANE MCCUNE

■ A well-written, social-serving book review that doesn't become an advertisement for the reviewer's ego can be both uplifting and delightful. Former columnist and editor for the *Province*, Shane McCune has consistently provided superior, smart and clear reviews of nonfiction. Here is just one.

MOST PEOPLE KNOW THE story of the Red Scare: after the war an irrational fear of communism led to witch hunts, censorship and purges. Police infiltrated unions and spied on civilians, due process was suspended, and lives were ruined or even lost.

Those crazy Americans, eh?

Actually, the events described above happened in Canada during and immediately after the First World War, 30 years before the McCarthy era. The years 1918 and 1919 were arguably the most chaotic, fearful and politically significant in Canada's history, yet few of us know much about them beyond references to the Spanish flu and the Winnipeg General Strike.

Into that breach steps North Vancouverite Daniel Francis, BC's best popular historian. His *Seeing Reds: The Red Scare of 1918–1919, Canada's First War on Terror*, is not only a solidly researched review of a neglected corner of our past but a gripping — and cautionary — tale.

For one thing, he reminds us that protecting civil liberties has never been a priority of the RCMP. Spying on civilians was not a dirty job foisted on the horsemen by politicians during the 1950s Cold War. It was part of its inheritance from the Royal Northwest Mounted Police (RNWMP), which embraced the task enthusiastically.

"[I]n the case of the RNWMP, it is probable that the force would not have survived if the Scare had not come along to give it a new reason for existing," Francis writes. So it's no surprise that, when asked to investigate the growing unrest and militancy among unions, the RNWMP ascribed it to leaders with unpronounceable names and suspicious accents, rather than to shrinking incomes, wretched working conditions, widespread unemployment and a very unpopular war.

That was also what the coalition government headed by Conservative Robert Borden wanted to hear. Under siege over conscription and a stalled economy, Borden was only too eager to redirect public anger toward the dreaded Reds (although Francis indicates the PM was not as hysterical about the threat as some of his ministers). And many labour leaders, especially in Western Canada, were in fact Bolshevik sympathizers, while others endorsed the Industrial Workers of the World (Wobblies) or the One Big Union. This radicalization of unionists sprang largely from their opposition to the war, a view not shared by mainstream labour groups back east, some of which even supported conscription.

It was also due to the wider political upheavals shaking the status quo around the world — the Russian Revolution, waves of immigration, militant unionism in Britain, anarchist violence in Germany and even the growth of left-wing movements in the US (Seattle's general strike preceded Winnipeg's by three months).

Having set the stage in his opening chapter, Dan Francis zooms in on the cast of characters, bringing them to life in quick, vivid sketches. On the left are bold and outspoken men and women excited to be part of a movement they believe will change the world for the better.

On the right are employers, politicians, police and war veterans determined to crush that movement by any means. Some are gripped by foolish fears, some are cynically exploiting such fears, and a few, such as national censor Ernest Chambers, are almost comical in their pomposity. Conflicts began to boil over in early 1918 as soldiers returning from the war demanded priority over non-combatants in the search for work, especially "enemy aliens." They were incensed by the anti-war campaigns of radical unionists, and there were violent clashes from one end of the country to the other.

Francis recaps the shooting of Albert "Ginger" Goodwin in the hills above Cumberland in the Comox Valley. That sparked Canada's first general strike in Vancouver on August 2, 1918, which in turn provoked mobs of veterans to attack labour halls and assault union leaders. (Goodwin is still a figure of controversy in Cumberland. In 1996 a nearby section of the Inland Island Highway was renamed Ginger Goodwin Way. The sign was repeatedly vandalized and eventually disappeared.)

Tory alarmists made wild claims about Bolshevik cells fomenting revolution in Canada under the direct control of puppeteers in Russia. Apart from the utter lack of evidence to back such claims, they were more than a little hypocritical in light of Canada's participation in efforts to undo the Russian Revolution.

A month after the Great War ended, the Canadian Siberian Expeditionary Force — including an RNWMP squadron — sailed for Vladivostok to fight the Bolsheviks. Its first skirmish took place in the streets of Victoria when some of the men mutinied. "Officers ordered other soldiers to remove their belts and whip the recalcitrants back into line," Francis writes. "Urged along at gunpoint, the mutineers eventually boarded the ship and the expeditionary force sailed for Siberia."

The climax of *Seeing Reds* is, of course, the Winnipeg General Strike. Francis' narrative here is almost cinematic in its pacing, its rapid switches among geographic and personal viewpoints and its sheer tension. Even though the reader knows how it will turn out — or perhaps because of that — each vignette adds to that tension.

The organizing council draws up last-minute plans, unaware that one of their number is an RNWMP plant. Women on both sides of the dispute pump gas, drive vehicles and generally keep essential services going. Sensationalist newspapers publish the vaguest of rumours, each one scarier than the last. Police "specials" find themselves surrounded by a hostile mob and have to be rescued. A wild storm hits the city, toppling trees and snapping trolley poles in an omen of the violence to come.

Of course the strike collapsed. It was followed by show trials of the leaders. The prosecution gained access to names of potential jurors and was able to stack the jury. At the trial of strike leader Bob Russell, RCMP officer Frank Zaneth, who had infiltrated the strike committee as organizer "Harry Blask," gave sensational testimony about conspiracies and ominous references to weapons — but nothing directly damning of Russell, whom he had never met. Even so, Russell was convicted, as were the other leaders. (Zaneth retired in 1951 as an assistant commissioner of the RCMP.)

On Boxing Day 1919, Russell was taken to Stony Mountain Penitentiary, where he served a year. Upon his release, according to one account cited by Francis, the presiding judge, then on his deathbed, asked to speak with Russell. He refused, saying: "Let him die with his guilty conscience."

Dan Francis notes one major difference between the first and second Red Scares: While McCarthy was chasing ghosts, the radical unionists of the first Scare "did pose a threat to the establishment." Not the church-burning, maiden-defiling, home-seizing threat cited by the shrillest of newspapers, but a determination to obtain better pay and working conditions and a say in the management of the economy — much scarier threats to employers and government. "In this sense the threat was real, and the Red Scare was less an illogical outbreak of paranoia than it was a response by the power elite to a challenge to its hegemony."

It's a cliché to say of a historical book that it is relevant today, but there's a reason why the subtitle refers to our "first war on terror." The parallels between Robert Borden's Canada and Stephen Harper's are inescapable: fear and hatred of alien immigrants (Bolsheviks then, Muslims now), ill-defined military operations overseas (Siberia, Afghanistan) and suppression of due process at home (reminiscent of the War Measures Act, secret trials).

At less than 300 pages, *Seeing Reds* manages to cover its subject with surprising thoroughness while remaining a brisk read. Every chapter offers details and insights that made me wonder, "Why didn't I learn this in school?"

[2011]

Wake Up and Smell
the Murder

■ In the same league as Shane McCune, novelist John Moore has set the
highest standard for reviews of fiction, first and foremost serving the reader
with astute observations and close reportage. Here he responds to the
debut of murder mystery novelist Glynis Whiting, who has introduced a
detective who solves crimes with a superior sense of smell.

IN HER FIRST, BUT probably not her last, murder mystery, *A Nose for
Death* (Thistledown), Glynis Whiting gets it right straight out of the gate.
It's hard to imagine a more perfect setting for a murder than a high school
reunion. After all, reuniting with classmates of twenty and thirty years
ago is largely an indulgence in what the Germans call *schadenfreude* — a
shameful pleasure in the misfortune of others — especially if you were
scorned by the cliques whose influence dominates a teenage social life
totally centred on school. Don't we all want to see the Bitch Prom Queen
packing fifty extra pounds of lard into a party dress and the Lothario of
the locker hall reduced to a beer-bellied, four-eyed schnook with a bald

spot you could land a jumbo jet on? We sniff at the details of their bank-ruptcies, affairs and divorces and substance-abuse issues like dogs around a ripe trash can.

In *A Nose for Death*, Joan Parker is the Girl-Least-Likely-to-Make-Good who actually did. Gifted with olfactory receptors a cut above the normal curve, Joan is one of those people, like winemakers and coffee tasters, who makes her living with her nose, analyzing and developing new flavours for a corporate food conglomerate. She's a corporate star and if her personal life is a little rocky as she enters middle age, it's still a long way from Madden, a town so small Kamloops was the big smoke, where she endured daily humiliations as the daughter of an improvident father who died early, forcing her mother to work as a chambermaid at the local hot sheets motel while Joan had to quit school to pull graveyard shifts at a gas bar owned by the father of the high school queen bee.

Since she didn't graduate and only later went back to school, driven by an interest in the chemistry of scents, Joan assumes her invitation is either a mistake or a ploy by someone to tap a successful alumnus for a donation. But for the chance of meeting her fellow high school outcast best friends, Hazel and Gabe, she'd leave Madden and those years in the cardboard box in the attic of memory where they belong. Whiting has tapped into the fact that the feelings you had for people when you were that age never die. Joan decides to go to the reunion, only to discover that the bad feelings you had about people when you were that age are just as persistent and the wounds are just as fresh — except that now they can prove fatal.

Her high school best friends, Hazel, now an out-front lesbian living in San Francisco, and Gabe, a former anarchist punk turned RCMP officer in charge of the Madden detachment, both have conflicted personal lives, and her old arch-enemy Marlena, gym-buffed in pursuit of perpetual youth, is still the spoiled-brat, queen bee of Madden society. Worst of all, the town's one-hit-wonder band, Rank, has re-formed to play the reunion dance. Roger, the band's singer whose failed attempt at a solo career has dragged him through every sewer between Madden and L.A. and back, is as odious as only a small town star that has sunk to the level he merits can be. He and Joan have history, as they say, and it's not the stuff of ro-mantic memoir.

By the time the first evening meet-and-greet winds up, scabs have been ripped off all over the room, and everyone's Inner Teenager has re-emerged, literally with a vengeance. After such an event, most people reassume adult form when they retreat to their hotel rooms, ask themselves what they were thinking when they accepted the invitation to an occasion so fraught with unresolved emotions, have a nightcap and go to bed. But for someone in the class, that's not going to be enough.

It's hard to review murder mysteries without inadvertently dropping spoilers. I'm not going to, because *A Nose for Death* is too good a read to wreck by giving away more of the plot. Whiting does an uncomfortably fine job of creating characters most of us born between 1950 and 1970 will recognize at a glance, especially if you grew up in a small town. She makes effective use of Agatha Christie's device of confining her characters to a small stage (isolated country house, moving train, tour group, etc.) without the obvious contrivance Dame Agatha and her imitators often resorted to in purely plot-driven mysteries. But modern mysteries, from Raymond Chandler to P.D. James and Ruth Rendell, are driven not by plot, but by character, and Whiting creates characters as familiar as the people we all went to school with.

Mystery writers fly under flags as false as their characters. Posing as mere purveyors of generic "entertainments" — a description Graham Greene used to describe some of his best novels — they have been our most perceptive and influential social critics. When the genre emerged in the late nineteenth and early twentieth century, mystery writers zeroed in on the class system in Britain and the meritocracy of money in North America, using genre fiction to expose "the best people on their worst behaviour" and captivated mass audiences for hours in a way no socialist demagogue could for five minutes. By the middle of the 20th century, mystery writers shifted their aim to society at large, exploring the dark emotional underside of

ordinary people, their own neighbours, under extreme stress, masked by the uniform civility of suburban life.

Baby Boomers are supposed to be the most self-obsessed, navel-gazing generation in history, yet surprisingly few novelists from that generation have made use of the plot device of having the chickens of political, social and sexual revolutions come home to roost. By using the device of the high school reunion, Whiting successfully captures and juxtaposes the changed values of two distinct eras in her characters' lives. Though Whiting makes use of Joan's "professional nose" as a plot device in the novel, she doesn't make it a cheap trick to resolve the plot. *A Nose for Death* is really about the people in a small town in BC, how they were in their youth, and what they have become as adults. Ultimately, that's much more interesting than the murder plot, and that's the sign of a good novel.

[2013]

Shakin' All Over:
Burlesque West

—◦ A.T.

■ All too often books by academics are given short shrift, but not so in *BC BookWorld* where academics receive as much coverage as poets. Here is a review of only one of countless worthwhile titles by BC academics.

AS UBC SOCIOLOGY professor Becki L. Ross will be the first to tell you, the storied Penthouse nightclub at 1019 Seymour Street merits a book of its own for the general public, and her book on the subject easily merited a feature review. Opened by the four Filippone brothers in 1947 the Penthouse used to attract up to 600 patrons per night as a "bottle club" (BYOB) to see the likes of Tony Bennett, Sophie Tucker, Sammy Davis Jr., Liberace, Harry Belafonte and Ella Fitzgerald.

At the Penthouse, Ross Filippone was general manager, Mickey ran the bar (natch), Jimmy was the maintenance man, lifelong bachelor Joe was the flashy front man, and sister Florence was the bookkeeper. The Filippones were discriminated against as Italians, for hiring black entertainers and for providing a safe haven for more than 100 prostitutes on any given night.

The city's "oldest stationary funhouse" started as one of precious few places in staid downtown Vancouver where one could get a decent steak. Police raided the place frequently, but patrons were given hiding places for their booze and there was usually a watchman on the roof to sound the alarm. The Filippones made ten failed applications for a legit liquor license before they succeeded in 1968.

Ten years later, *Sun* columnist Denny Boyd reflected, "It was the place to go after hours to get a steak, mixer for your bottle, see a show, run into a friend or find a hooker. Make no mistake about it, hookers came to The Penthouse. So did other club owners, musicians, lawyers, safecrackers, corporation presidents, Hollywood starlets, cheating husbands, stock-brokers, school principals, gamblers, plainclothes RCMP surveillance teams, PTA presidents, surgeons, drug-users, short-order cooks and — I suspect — the odd man of the cloth."

Becki L. Ross' *Burlesque West: Showgirls, Sex and Sin in Postwar Vancouver* (University of Toronto Press) necessarily chronicles the colourful Penthouse but her scope is much more ambitious and informative than mere nostalgia or rear-view voyeurism. Glitzier, westside hangouts like Isy's and The Cave were not allowed to overshadow the eastside clubs such as the New Delhi Cabaret and the Harlem Nocturne run by Choo Choo Williams and Ernie King. We learn that as early as 1945, headliner Yvette Dare at the Beacon Theatre had a trained parrot named Jeta that helped her disrobe on stage. Her show was billed as a Balinese dance to the bird god.

Cumulatively, *Burlesque West* is a superbly researched chronicle of how Vancouver, a city with some of North America's most stringent and puritanical liquor laws for decades, became one of the hotspots for stripping in the 1970s and 1980s. For the record, the Club Zanzibar (formerly Torch Cabaret), the Factory and Café Kobenhavn introduced so-called "bottomless" dancing in the fall of 1971. Eventually even Isy's nightclub on Georgia Street would become Isy's Strip City.

Burlesque West is a rare academic work, groundbreaking, accessible, lucid and completely serious. The fact that its author generated a minor stir when she received a major research grant to undertake the study merely proves the need for a frank and public examination of burlesque and its offshoots in the first place.

G-strings came off with the election of the NDP in 1972. The musical *Hair* had played in Toronto, with full nudity, and no charges had been laid. Hey, if Toronto could handle it. . . .

Café Kobenhavn, at 968 Main Street, was run by the Satan's Angels biker gang. By 1972, when dancers and staff were charged with presenting an obscene performance, the *Province* entertainment reporter, Michael Walsh, testified on the club's behalf by noting he had counted 29 females and 111 males sunbathing nude at Wreck Beach. The genie, or Jeannie, was out of the bottle.

So-called peeler clubs mushroomed. By 1975, there were thirty locales featuring full nudity in Vancouver, as well as countless venues in the Lower Mainland, such as No. 5 Orange, Austin, American, St. Helen's, Royal, Niagara, St. Regis, Drake, Marr, Nelson Place, Balmoral, Castle, New Fountain, Fraser Arms, Marble Arch, Piccadilly, Yale, Cobalt, Dufferin, Vanport, Barn, Cecil and The Factory.

Just as television had threatened the demise of The Penthouse in the fifties and sixties, back when folks could stay at home and watch Dean Martin and Jerry Lewis on *The Ed Sullivan Show* for free, exotic dancers in beer parlours for the price of a beer made for even stiffer competition than TV. Ross Filippone told Becki Ross: "The hotels started to bring in top-line girls. . . . They were giving the public what they wanted. No cover charge." The Penthouse and other nightclubs had a cover charge and could stay open only from 7 p.m. to 2 a.m., whereas a beer parlour in a hotel could have dancers from noon to 2 a.m.

As St. Regis Hotel manager Larry Thiesson told the *Province*, "hotels aren't churches." And so it was that Vancouver — somewhat bizarrely — suddenly became one of the best places in North America to find bump & grind.

Ross' academic approach, tinged with feminism, does not overlook the fascinating range of characters, such as notorious entrepreneur Gary Taylor, now in his late sixties. Taylor started his career as a teenage drummer backing dancers at clubs like the Smilin' Buddha, and at the PNE's girlie shows. "It was rumoured that Taylor was a smooth, fast-talking operator who bet strangers on the street that he could get a woman to take her clothes off on his stage," Ross writes. "A long-time friend joked that Taylor could talk a nun into going on stage."

Most of the larger-than-life club owners such as Ernie King, Ross Fillipone and Richard Walters (living in California) reached old age. Isy Walters died in his club of a heart attack. Joe Filippone died in his club with a bullet in his head.

Somewhat nostalgic for the olden days, and always admiring of the artistry and courage of the performers, Ross in her examination of burlesque as a business proves equally engaging. We learn that when top-line American dancers such as Sally Rand, Gypsy Rose Lee, Ricki Covette, Lili St. Cyr and Tempest Storm performed in Vancouver during the 1950s and 1960s, they were earning up to $5,000 per week even after they turned forty years of age. "While most female service workers were paid low wages, earning 57 percent of what men earned doing similar work," Ross writes, "only a small number of women in corporations and in the professions of law and medicine matched the income of 'white features' following World War II."

Erotic dancing can be a profession. It's not perhaps the oldest profession, but perhaps close to it. And for a few decades, Vancouver, like it or not, was a hip-swivelling and gyrating Mecca for women who plied their skin trade as dancers. And through it all, The Penthouse remains open at the heart of the city, sixty years young, a bastion of burlesque.

In a nutshell, Ross has combined thorough research with a clear-eyed sensibility that looks beyond "a puritan ideology that is at once fascinated and repulsed by female nudity and sexuality" to prove that erotic dancers who work full time deserve to have their vocation respected and appreciated *as work*.

[2010]

The Fight to Save the Earth, 1970–1979

— A.T.

◼ Possibly British Columbia's greatest gift to the world is Greenpeace. Thank goodness — and thank greenness — that this fantastical, life-affirming, death-defying, heart-stoppingly erratic and distinctly British Columbian story of flawed heroes, the power of belief and ballsy propaganda, all for a good cause, has been gathered responsibly and well, into one reliable volume. *Greenpeace* (Raincoast), by Rex Weyler, goes alongside Robert Hunter's version of events, *The Greenpeace to Amchitka: An Environmental Odyssey* (Arsenal Pulp), with photographs by Robert Keziere.

IF *GREENPEACE* COULD BE made into a movie, it could only be directed by Peter Jackson as a trilogy. In the early '70s, the environmental protest movement was Tolkien for real. Even at the time, Hunter referred to Vancouver as the Shire and he dubbed their crusty-but-trusty Captain John Cormack "Lord of the Piston Rings." It all started when a bunch of boys went on a quest on a converted halibut seiner. Amid the pot smoke and rhetoric, the depths of Mordor were somewhere in the Aleutian Islands.

Ben Metcalfe (the "Alpha Intellectual") manipulated the world media, and Bob Hunter launched his "mind bombs." It was Hunter who coined the slogan "Don't Make a Wave" to galvanize global fears that a tidal wave might ensue if the US succeeded in detonating a 5.2 megaton hydrogen bomb in Alaska as planned.

Single women weren't allowed on the first protest voyage to Amchitka simply because the old fashioned skipper of the *Phyllis Cormack* (named after his wife Phyllis Cormack) owned the boat, and he was implacable. Hunter dubbed the crew "Captain Cormack's Lonely Hearts Club Band." At first the boys happily debated the merits of Herbert Marcuse while listening to Moody Blues and Beethoven, but they were soon perplexed because somebody on board was stealing chocolate. Frequently seasick, they worried that one of their kind was a CIA operative. For two days they escaped detection by the US Coast Guard simply because they had steered too far in the wrong direction. The captain terrorized them. The crew became divided. Mechanics vs. mystics. Canadians vs. Americans.

Jeez, did all that stuff *really* happen? Yes, Virginia, a bunch of guys really did get into an old fish boat in 1971 and sail towards the Bering Sea to prevent the evil Richard Nixon and the US military from detonating an experimental blast 400 times greater than the one that levelled Hiroshima.

Few people recall that there was a second Greenpeace vessel, the *Greenpeace Too*, that made it into the danger zone of Amchitka, only to have the bomb explode anyway. Just as Steve Fonyo outran Terry Fox, succeeding in crossing the country on one leg, the contributions of that second (more courageous? more foolhardy?) crew are barely mentioned in Weyler's account, or elsewhere.

The US Atomic Energy Commission had already detonated two previous explosions in Alaska in 1965 and 1969. Nixon eventually won the Amchitka battle of wills but he lost the propaganda war of beliefs. The largest man-made explosion in history occurred on November 6, 1971, but from those deadly ashes there arose Greenpeace, an environmental success story so charming and persuasive that even the likes of W.A.C. Bennett jumped onto the bandwagon.

It all started accidentally on purpose.

Once upon a very different time — when the word ecology was new — some 1950s style disarmament types in Vancouver, led by Jewish Quakers Irving & Dorothy Stowe and their fellow American transplants Jim & Marie Bohlen, melded with 1960s-style environmental activists who were inspired by headstrong journalists Ben Metcalfe (CBC Radio), Bob Hunter (*Vancouver Sun*) and Bob Cummings (*Georgia Straight*) — the Huey, Duey and Luey of Left Coast idealism — and, literally in their wake, a save-the-planet movement called Greenpeace was born.

Along the way these visionaries were aided and abetted by Joni Mitchell, Pierre Berton & Gordon Lightfoot, a homegrown ecologist named Patrick Moore, a gutsy activist named Paul Watson (later Moore's nemesis), Brigitte Bardot, a heroic and stubborn sailor named Paul McTaggart (who dismissed Metcalfe as a fraud), a whale named Skana, quixotic aquarium cetologist Paul Spong, agitprop comic Wavy Gravy, the Pope, Jean-Paul Sartre, Dan McLeod, Yippie founder Paul Krassner and . . . well, there are too many to mention them all.

Weyler's composite history *Greenpeace* reads like a hip James Michener novel, replete with fabricated snippets of conversation and scientific asides. It owes much to the records and opinions of the late Ben Metcalfe and Bob Hunter, both of whom are writers who have left a trail of quotes and opinions. Hunter's *Warriors of the Rainbow* appears to be the main source for Weyler's version of that remarkable first voyage.

Weyler's diplomatic attempt to make a definitive volume probably pulls more than a few punches, but he gives credit to the importance of some lesser-known activists such as Walrus Oakenbough and hippie Rod Waring, founder of the Rocky Rococo Theatre Company. Waring led an important (and successful) camp-in protest against plans for a hotel complex at the entrance to Stanley Park and he was the first Greenpeace victim of police brutality when he was beaten in Paris, having chained himself inside Notre Dame Cathedral. The *Georgia Straight*'s key correspondent Bob Cummings is given short shrift, perhaps because Weyler arrived in Vancouver as a draft evader in June of 1972 and he wasn't here to appreciate the extent to which the *Georgia Straight* created the zeitgeist. Bob Cummings committed suicide in 1987, unheralded.

Similarly, Weyler's coverage of the 1970 benefit concert omits reference to the bizarre moment when Phil Ochs, the most potent American protest singer of his era, stepped onto the stage at Pacific Coliseum and acknowledged Canada's newly implemented War Measures Act. "Geez, I've never played in a police state before," Ochs quipped, only to be booed by his audience. They came for entertainment, not politics.

But by the time Hunter/Frodo, Weyler and the stalwart Moore gather in an Amsterdam bar and accept the dissolution of the Greenpeace Foundation in 1979, toasting Captain Cormack in the process, we feel we've been taken on a long, magical journey, grateful for the experience. All that's really missing is a soundtrack and an index.

[2004]

Be Strong. Be Steadfast.
Be True.

⟿ CHIEF JOE GOSNELL

■ Wearing a red-and-black button blanket over his business suit, Chief Joe Gosnell arrived at the Legislature on December 2, 1998, to deliver the following historic speech to launch debate on *Bill 51: The Nisga'a Final Agreement Act*. He called it a triumph "because the treaty proves beyond all doubt that negotiations — not lawsuits, not blockades, not violence — are the most effective, most honourable way to resolve Aboriginal issues in this country." The reproduction of this speech in the Summer 2001 issue of *BC BookWorld* marked the publication of Alex Rose's *Spirit Dance at Meziadin* (Harbour 2001), a book that gives the full story of why and how the Nisga'a and Chief Joe Gosnell finally won control of their land, alongside photos from Gary Fiegehen and Nisga'a archives. (The speech has been edited for length).

IN 1887, MY ANCESTORS made an epic journey from the Nass River here to Victoria's inner harbour. Determined to settle the Land Question, they were met by a premier who barred them from the legislature. He was blunt. Premier Smithe rejected all our aspirations to settle the Land

Question. Then he made this pronouncement, and I quote: "When the white man first came among you, you were little better than wild beasts of the field." Wild beasts of the field! Little wonder then, that this brutal racism was soon translated into narrow policies which plunged British Columbia into a century of darkness for the Nisga'a and other Aboriginal people.

Like many colonists of the day, Premier Smithe did not know, or care to know, that the Nisga'a is an old nation, as old as any in Europe. From time immemorial, our oral literature, passed down from generation to generation, records the story of the way the Nisga'a people were placed on earth, entrusted with the care and protection of our land. Through the ages, we lived a settled life in villages along the Nass River. We lived in large, cedar-planked houses, fronted with totem poles depicting the great heraldry and the family crests of our nobility. We thrived from the bounty of the sea, the river, the forest, and the mountains.

We governed ourselves according to *Ayuuk̲hl Nisga'a*, the code of our own strict and ancient laws of property ownership, succession and civil order. Our first encounters with Europeans were friendly. We welcomed strange visitors, visitors who never left. The Europeans also valued their encounters with us. They thought we were fair and tough entrepreneurs and, no doubt today, negotiators. In 1832, traders from the Hudson's Bay Company found us living, in their words, "in two-storey wooden houses the equal of any in Europe." For a time, we continued to prosper.

But there were dark days to come. Between the late-1700s and the mid-1800s, the Nisga'a people, like so many other coastal nations of the time, were devastated by European diseases such as smallpox, measles and fevers. Our population, once 30,000, dwindled to about 800 people. Today, I am pleased to report, our population is growing again. Today, we number 5,500 people.

We took to heart the promises of King George III, set out in the Royal Proclamation of 1763, that our lands would not be taken without our permission. We continued to follow our *Ayuuk̲hl*, our code of laws. We vowed to obey the white man's laws, too, and we expected him to obey his own law — and respect ours.

But the Europeans did not obey their own laws, and continued to trespass on our lands. The King's governments continued to take our lands from us, until we were told that all of our lands had come to belong to the Crown, and even the tiny bits of land that enclosed our villages were not ours, but belonged to the government. Still we kept faith that the rule of law would prevail one day, that justice would be done. That one day, the Land Question would be settled fairly and honourably.

In 1913, the Nisga'a Land Committee drafted a petition to London. The petition contained a declaration of our traditional land ownership and governance and it contained the critical affirmation that, in the new British colony, our land ownership would be respected. In part the petition said:

"We are not opposed to the coming of the white people into our territory, provided this be carried out justly and in accordance with the British principles embodied in the Royal Proclamation. Therefore as we expect the Aboriginal rights which we claim should be established by the decision of His Majesty's Privy Council, we would be prepared to take a moderate and reasonable position. In that event, while claiming the right to decide for ourselves, the terms upon which we would deal with our territory, we would be willing that all matters outstanding between the province and ourselves should be finally adjusted by some equitable method to be agreed upon which should include representation of the Indian Tribes upon any Commission which might then be appointed."

The above statement was unanimously adopted at a meeting of the Nisga'a Nation or Tribe of Indians held at the village of Gingolx on the twenty-second day of January, 1913. Sadly, this was not to be the case.

Also in 1913, Duncan Campbell Scott became deputy superintendent of Indian Affairs. His narrow vision of assimilation dominated federal Aboriginal policy for years and years to come and was later codified as the *Indian Act*. Mr. Scott said, "I want to get rid of the Indian problem. Our objective is to continue until there is not a single Indian in Canada that has not been absorbed into the body politic and there is no Indian question." One of this man's earliest efforts was to undermine the influence of the Nisga'a petition to London and to deflect attention away from political action. Still, the situation of the Nisga'a worsened. In 1927 Canada passed a law to prevent us from pursuing our land claims, from hiring lawyers to plead our case. At the same time, our central institution of tribal government, the potlatch system (*yuukw*), was outlawed by an Act of Parliament. It was against the law for us to give presents to one another during our ceremonies, which our laws instructed us to do. It was even made illegal for us to sing, to dance.

But still we never gave up. And then finally, under the leadership of President Emeritus Frank Calder, the Nisga'a Land Committee was re-born as the Nisga'a Tribal Council in 1955. In 1968, we took our Land Question to the BC Supreme Court. We lost but appealed to the Supreme Court of Canada, where in 1973 — in what is now known as the Calder case — the judges ruled that Aboriginal title existed prior to Confederation. This initiated the modern-day process of land claims negotiations. The government of Canada agreed it was best to negotiate modern-day treaties. Canada agreed it was time to build a new relationship, based on trust, respect and the rule of law. In time, as you well know, Madame Speaker, the province of British Columbia came to the negotiating table as well. For the past twenty-five years, in good faith, the Nisga'a struggled to negotiate this treaty and finally, it was initialled in August in our village of Gitlakdamix.

How the world changed. Two days ago and one hundred and eleven years after Smithe's rejection, I walked up the steps of this legislature as the sound of Nisga'a drumming and singing filled the rotunda. To the Nisga'a people, it was a joyous sound, the sound of freedom. What does *freedom* mean? I looked it up in the dictionary. It means "the state or condition of being free, the condition of not being under another's control; the power to do, say, or think as one pleases."

Our people have enjoyed the hospitality and warmth of this legislature, this capital city, its sites and its people — in churches, schools, malls, streets and public places. Our people have been embraced, welcomed and congratulated by the people of British Columbia, Madame Speaker. People sometimes wonder why we have struggled so long to sign a treaty. Why, we are asked, did our elders and elected officials dedicate their lives to a resolution of the Land Question? What is it about a treaty? To us, a treaty is a sacred instrument. It represents an understanding between distinct cultures and shows respect for each other's way of life. We know we are here for a long time together. A treaty stands as a symbol of high idealism in a divided world. That is why we have fought so long, and so hard. I have been asked, has it been worth it? Yes, a resounding yes. But, believe me, it has been a long and hard-fought battle. Some may have heard us say that a generation of Nisga'a men and women has grown old at the negotiating table. Sadly, it is very true.

Let me share some personal history. When I began this process I was a young man. When I first became involved in our Tribal Council, I was twenty-five years old. Now I am sixty-three. Today, my hair is grey. The terms of six prime ministers chart the years I have grown old at the negotiating table. . . .

We are not naïve. We know that some people do not want this treaty. We know there are naysayers, some sitting here today. We know there are some who say Canada and BC are "giving" us too much. And a few who want to re-open negotiations in order to "give" us less. Others — still upholding the values of Smithe and Scott — are practising willful ignorance. This colonial attitude is fanning the flames of fear and ignorance in this province and reigniting a poisonous attitude so familiar to Aboriginal people.

But these are desperate tactics doomed to fail. By playing politics with the aspirations of Aboriginal people, these naysayers are blighting the promise of the Nisga'a Treaty — not only for us, but for non-Aboriginal people as well. Because, Madame Speaker, this is about people. We are not numbers. In this legislative debate, you will be dealing with the lives of our people, with the futures of our individual people. This is about the legitimate aspirations of people no longer willing to step aside or be marginalized. We intend to be free and equal citizens, Madame Speaker. . . .

Now, on the eve of the fiftieth anniversary of the Declaration of Human Rights, this legislature embarks on a great debate about Aboriginal rights. The Nisga'a people welcome that debate — one of the most important in the modern history of British Columbia. And we have every confidence that elected members of this legislature will look beyond narrow politics to correct a shameful and historical wrong. I ask every Honourable Member to search their heart deeply and to allow the light of our message to guide their decision.

We have worked for justice for more than a century. Now, it is time to ratify the Nisga'a Treaty, for Aboriginal and non-Aboriginal people to come together and write a new chapter in the history of our nation, our province, our country and, indeed, the world. The world is our witness. Be strong. Be steadfast. Be true.

(2001)

Afterword

—◦ ALAN TWIGG

I'VE MET MANY noteworthy people since I started publishing *BC Book-World*, such as Joni Mitchell, Leonard Cohen and the enigmatic founder of Belize, George Price, but these people remain secondary. My life has been much more enriched by the thousands of BC authors I've come across running *BC BookWorld*. I am humbled and inspired by the constant influx of their intelligence.

After twenty-five years, I realize my job is akin to being a turnstile operator at Ellis Island, processing entrants. I am a gatekeeper for literature. It's not glamorous. I lick the stamps, I do the banking. But my colleague David Lester and I are happy to be useful, keeping track of each and every BC book and author — making sure nobody gets forgotten.

As of the writing of this sentence, there are at least 10,554 listings on our abcbookworld reference site, for and about BC authors. Seeing the books by these people is a daily tonic. (If you are down in the mouth about anything, there is a simple antidote: Learn something.) Every day I regard the task of producing *BC BookWorld* as a privilege because I get to learn so much. Witnessing the outpouring of fine books about the place I was born, as a fifth-generation Vancouverite, provides me with a foundation worth the perseverance required.

If ever you want to generate silence in room of supposedly educated people, just ask them to name the first premier of BC (John McCreight) or the first European mariner we can be certain reached BC waters (Juan Pérez — although the evidence that Juan de Fuca arrived before him is very strong). The lovable historian Chuck Davis used to go into schools and show kids a photo of George Vancouver and they *always* guessed it was George Washington.

It is amazing how little most people know about British Columbia. That's mainly because, until recently, the majority of people in BC were born outside the province. As much as *BC BookWorld* might appear to function chiefly as a literary periodical, its mandate becomes clearer if you regard *BC BookWorld* as an educational newspaper. It is my job to print the cultural news that is refracted in books.

If you are an anthropologist travelling to the heart of Borneo in 1800, and you hold up a mirror to people in loin cloths and they see their reflection for the first time, those tribesmen are going to get excited. *BC Book-World* is designed and written to serve as a cultural mirror in much the same way. We begin by assuming most people know next to nothing.

I grew up wearing Cowichan Indian sweaters. I knew the Trail Smoke-Eaters were world champions. I knew who Percy Williams was. Ma Murray. Flyin' Phil Gaglardi. *Three Against the Wildnerness* by Eric Collier. Ripple Rock. Roderick Haig-Brown. By 1987, it wasn't difficult to see that *BC BookWorld* was a necessity — having been involved in the creation of the BC Book Prizes in 1985, and the first Jessie Richardson Theatre Awards before that. Since then we have created more literary prizes, as well as the abcbookworld reference site; and now there's a new *BC Book-Look* daily news service.

We hold up as many mirrors as we can.

Vancouver is Vladivostok and Toronto is Moscow. If people in Moscow don't give a damn about what is happening in Vladivostok, the Vladivostokians mustn't be surprised or upset. It's up to everyone in Vladivostok to build their own institutions. The Torontonians have long done a good job trying to care about the Vancouverites, but the Vancouverites must mature and get rid of their parents. We have to grow up and grow our own cultural institutions.

Pierre Berton once told me that Canadians value institutions and Americans value individuals. I think that is far less true today than in the mid-1980s when we were talking, but Berton's simple and big idea has served as a compass to set our course. From the first issue I have sought to make *BC BookWorld* into a cultural given, to institutionalize it, like the CBC. If I don't put my name in it, except in the masthead, and I don't give myself a column, it's not for lack of ego; it's pragmatism. It's all about the reader holding that mirror.

John Fowles, somewhere in his novel *Daniel Martin*, wrote a line that I've never forgotten: "To draw attention to anything is to glorify it." My job, with the essential help of designer David Lester, is to glorify BC books and authors by simply drawing attention to them. Telling people what to read, or what to think, is a trap into which the literary aristocracy constantly falls, while degrading their enemies and promoting their friends. The public justifiably turns away from such elitist tomfoolery. That's not our style.

If I want to attract as many readers as possible, it's simply dumb to tell other people what they should think. The public quite rightly abhors such condescension. At *BC BookWorld* we strive to let the general public decide what is good and bad. If, for instance, you have a grandfather who loves fly fishing and he lives in the Okanagan, you will be pleased to buy him *The Gilley* for Christmas and *he* can be the person who passes judgment on its value as a fishing guide.

But first you have to learn *The Gilley* exists.

Only connect. Not all bureaucrats have understood this populist agenda — to reach as many people as possible, with as much information as possible, about as many BC books as possible — but the Canada Council, thank goodness, has been consistently supportive. The majority of revenues for *BC BookWorld* are self-generated by ads, largely because *BC BookWorld* has more readers than any other independent Canadian publication about books. We *know* people like *BC BookWorld*, and that knowledge makes us deeply grateful and happy.

We expect to carry on. Just in case all the current e-hype is for real, we have newly created *BC BookLook* as a digital equivalent of the newspaper. Meanwhile, on behalf of Dave — who did the cartoons — and myself, I hope you have enjoyed this collection, and thanks for being readers.